CERTIFICATION CIRCLE™

MOUS

Microsoft Word 2002

Katherine Pinard

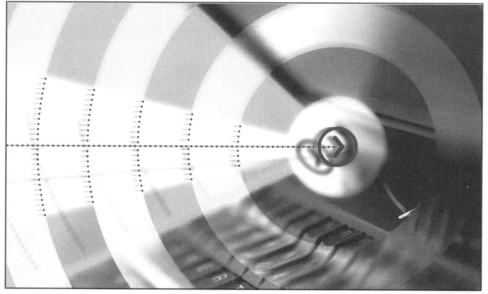

CORE

APPROVED COURSEWARE

COURSE
TECHNOLOGY

THOMSON LEARNING

Australia • Canada • Mexico • Singapore • Spain • United Kingdom • United States

MOUS Microsoft Word 2002

CERTIFICATION CIRCLE™ CORE

Katherine Pinard

Managing Editor:
Nicole Jones Pinard

Product Managers:
Debbie Masi
Julia Healy

Editorial Assistant:
Christina Kling Garrett

Production Editor:
Debbie Masi

Contributing Author:
Carol Cram

Developmental Editors:
Laurie PiSierra, Kim Crowley

Composition House:
GEX Publishing Services

QA Manuscript Reviewers:
Nicole Ashton, John Freitas,
Jeff Schwartz, Alex White

Book Designers:
Joseph Lee, black fish design

Thank You, Advisory Board!

This book is a result of the hard work and dedication by authors, editors, and more than 30 instructors focused on Microsoft Office and MOUS certification. These instructors formed our Certification Circle Advisory Board. We looked to them to flesh out our original vision and turn it into a sound pedagogical method of instruction. In short, we asked them to partner with us to create *the* book for preparing for a MOUS Exam. And, now we wish to thank them for their contributions and expertise.

ADVISORY BOARD MEMBERS:

Linda Amergo	Old Westbury
Shellie Besharse	Mississippi County Community College
Margaret Britt	Copiah Lincoln Community College
Becky Burt	Copiah Lincoln Community College
Judy Cameron	Spokane Community College
Elizabeth T. De Arazoza	Miami-Dade Community College
Susan Dozier	Tidewater Community College
Dawna Dewire	Babson College
Pat Evans	J. Sargent Reynolds
Susan Fry	Boise State University
Joyce Gordon	Babson College
Steve Gordon	Babson College
Pat Harley	Howard Community College
Rosanna Hartley	Western Piedmont Community College
Eva Hefner	St. Petersburg Junior College
Becky Jones	Richland College
Mali Jones	Johnson and Wales University
Angie McCutcheon	Washington State Community College
Barbara Miller	Indiana University
Carol Milliken	Kellogg Community College
Maureen Paparella	Monmouth University
Mike Puopolo	Bunker Hill Community College
Kathy Proittei	Essex Community College
Pamela M. Randall	Unicity Network
Theresa Savarese	San Diego City College
Barbara Sherman	Buffalo State
Kathryn Surles	Salem Community College
Beth Thomas	Hagerstown Community College
Barbara Webber	Northern Essex Community College
Jean Welsh	Lansing Community College
Lynn Wermers	North Shore Community College
Sherry Young	Kingwood College

Preface

Welcome to the *CERTIFICATION CIRCLE SERIES*. Each book in this series is designed with one thing in mind: preparing you to pass a Microsoft Office User Specialist (MOUS) exam. This strict focus allows you to target the skills you need to be successful. You will not need to study anything extra—it's like getting a peek at the exam before you take it! Read on to learn more about how the book is organized and how you will get the most out of it.

Table of Contents
This book is organized around the MOUS exam objectives. Each Skill on the exam is taught on two facing pages with text on the left and figures on the right. This also makes for a terrific reference; if you want to brush up on a few skills, it's easy to find the ones you're looking for.

Getting Started Chapter
Each book begins with a Getting Started Chapter. This Chapter contains skills that are *not* covered on the exam but the authors felt were vital to understanding the software. The content in this chapter varies from application to application.

Skill Overview
Each skill starts with a paragraph explaining the concept and how you would use it. These are clearly written and concise.

File Open Icon
We provide a realistic project file for every skill. And, it's in the form you need it in order to work through the steps; there's no wasted time building the file before you can work with it.

Skill Steps
The Steps required to perform the skill appear on the left page with what you type in green text.

Tips
We provide tips specific to the skill or how the skill is tested on the exam.

Skill Set 8
Integrating with Other Applications

Import Data to Access
Import Data from an Excel Workbook

You can import data into an Access database from several file formats, including an Excel workbook or another Access, FoxPro, dBase, or Paradox database. It is not uncommon for a user to enter a list of data into Excel and later decide to convert that data into an Access database, because the user wants to use Access's extensive form or report capabilities or wants multiple people to be able to use the data at the same time. (An Access database is inherently **multi-user**; many people can enter and update data at the same time.) Since the data in an Excel workbook is structured similarly to data in an Access table datasheet, you can easily import data from an Excel workbook into an Access database by using the **Import Spreadsheet Wizard**.

Activity Steps
Classes01.mdb

1. Click **File** on the menu bar, point to **Get External Data**, then click **Import**

2. Navigate to the drive and folder where your Project Files are stored, click the **Files of type list arrow**, click **Microsoft Excel**, click **Instructors**, then click **Import** to start the Import Spreadsheet Wizard
   See Figure 8-1.

3. Select the **First Row Contains Column Headings check box**, then click **Next**

4. Click **Next** to indicate that you want to create a new table, then click **Next** to not specify field changes

5. Click the **Choose my own primary key option button** to set InstructorID as the primary key field, then click **Next**

6. Type **Instructors** in the Import to Table box, click **Finish**, then click **OK**

7. Double-click **Instructors** to open it in Datasheet View
   See Figure 8-2. Imported data works the same way as any other table of data in a database.

8. Close the Instructors table

tip

Step 4
You can also import Excel workbook data into an existing table if the field names used in the Excel workbook match the field names in the Access table.

98   Certification Circle

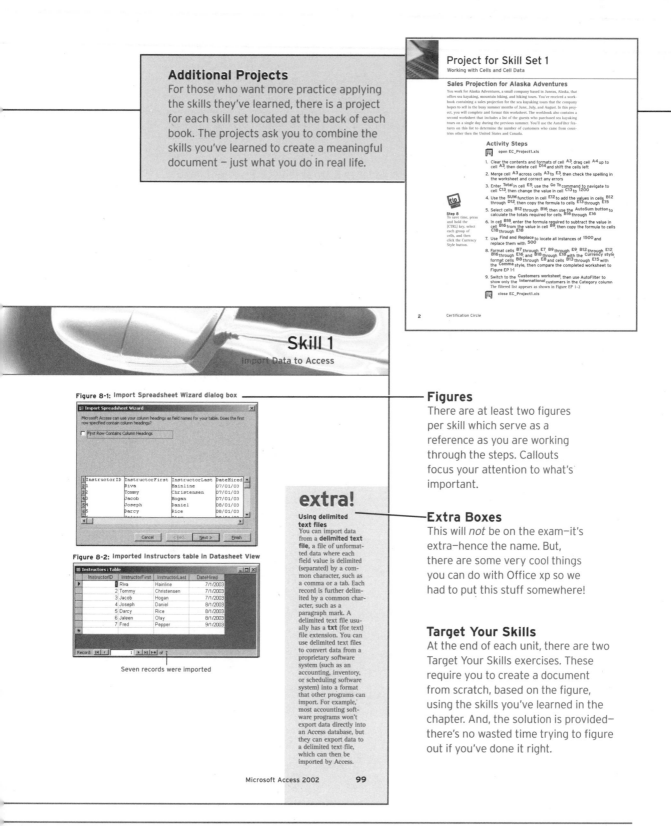

Additional Projects

For those who want more practice applying the skills they've learned, there is a project for each skill set located at the back of each book. The projects ask you to combine the skills you've learned to create a meaningful document – just what you do in real life.

Skill 1
Import Data to Access

Figure 8-1: Import Spreadsheet Wizard dialog box

Figures

There are at least two figures per skill which serve as a reference as you are working through the steps. Callouts focus your attention to what's important.

Figure 8-2: Imported Instructors table in Datasheet View

Seven records were imported

extra!

Using delimited text files

You can import data from a **delimited text file**, a file of unformatted data where each field value is delimited (separated) by a common character, such as a comma or a tab. Each record is further delimited by a common character, such as a paragraph mark. A delimited text file usually has a **txt** (for text) file extension. You can use delimited text files to convert data from a proprietary software system (such as an accounting, inventory, or scheduling software system) into a format that other programs can import. For example, most accounting software programs won't export data directly into an Access database, but they can export data to a delimited text file, which can then be imported by Access.

Extra Boxes

This will *not* be on the exam—it's extra—hence the name. But, there are some very cool things you can do with Office xp so we had to put this stuff somewhere!

Target Your Skills

At the end of each unit, there are two Target Your Skills exercises. These require you to create a document from scratch, based on the figure, using the skills you've learned in the chapter. And, the solution is provided—there's no wasted time trying to figure out if you've done it right.

Additional Resources

There are many resources available with this book—both free and for a nominal fee. Please see your sales representative for more information. The resources available with this book are:

INSTRUCTOR'S MANUAL

Available as an electronic file, the Instructor's Manual is quality-assurance tested and includes unit overviews, lecture topics, solutions to all lessons and projects, and extra Target Your Skills. The Instructor's Manual is available on the Instructor's Resource Kit CD-ROM, or you can download if from www.course.com.

FACULTY ONLINE COMPANION

You can browse this textbook's password protected site to obtain the Instructor's Manual, Solution Files, Project Files, and any updates to the text. Contact your Customer Service Representative for the site address and password.

PROJECT FILES

Project Files contain all of the data that students will use to complete the lessons and projects. A Readme file includes instructions for using the files. Adopters of this text are granted the right to install the Project Files on any stand-alone computer or network. The Project Files are available on the Instructor's Resource Kit CD-ROM, the Review Pack, and can also be downloaded from www.course.com.

SOLUTION FILES

Solution Files contain every file students are asked to create or modify in the lessons and projects. A Help file on the Instructor's Resource Kit includes information for using the Solution Files.

FIGURE FILES

Figure Files contain all the figures from the book in bitmap format. Use the figure files to create transparency masters or in a PowerPoint presentation.

SAM, SKILLS ASSESSMENT MANAGER FOR MICROSOFT OFFICE XP SM^{xp}

SAM is the most powerful Office XP assessment and reporting tool that will help you gain a true understanding of your students' proficiency in Microsoft Word, Excel, Access, and PowerPoint 2002.

TOM, TRAINING ONLINE MANAGER FOR MICROSOFT OFFICE XP TOM

TOM is Course Technology's MOUS-approved training tool for Microsoft Office XP. Available via the World Wide Web and CD-ROM, TOM allows students to actively learn Office XP concepts and skills by delivering realistic practice through both guided and self-directed simulated instruction.

Certification Circle Series, SAM, and TOM: the true training and assessment solution for Office XP.

Contents

MOUS Microsoft Word 2002

CERTIFICATION CIRCLE™ *CORE*

Getting Started

Getting Started with Word 2002

Skill List

1. Start and exit Word
2. Understand toolbars
3. Understand task panes
4. Open and close documents
5. Work with more than one open document
6. Navigate in the document window
7. Understand views
8. Save the files you create
9. Use smart tags
10. Get help

Microsoft Word is a **word-processing program,** a program that makes it easy to enter and manipulate text in documents. A **document** is any file that you create using Word.

Before you can start creating your own documents, you need to learn a few fundamentals about working with Word, including how to start and exit the program, open and close documents, navigate in a document, open and close task panes, change views, save files, use smart tags, and use Help.

Getting Started

Start and Exit Word

Before you can create documents, you need to start Word. In this lesson, you will learn how to start and exit the Word program. When you start Word, you open the Word program window and a blank document window.

Activity Steps

tip

Step 5
You can also click Exit on the File menu to exit Word.

1. Click the **Start button**  on the Windows taskbar

2. Point to **Programs**
   See Figure GS-1.

3. Click **Microsoft Word**

4. If necessary, click the **Maximize button** in the Word program window title bar
   See Figure GS-2.

5. Click the **Close button** in the program window title bar

---

extra!

Understanding filename extensions
Each Windows program uses a different **filename extension**, the three letters that follow a period after the filename itself. The unique extensions identify each document's file type. Word creates document files with the **.doc** file extension. Word also uses the extension **.dot** to identify template files, documents that have built-in formatting that you use as a starting point for creating a new document. Word can also create and open files with the extension **.htm**, which identifies Hyper Text Markup Language (HTML) files, the file type that Web pages use.

Figure GS-1: Starting Word

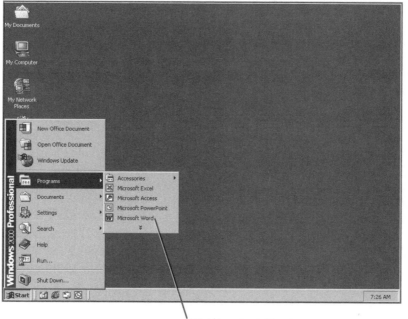

Click to start Word

Figure GS-2: Word program window

File menu

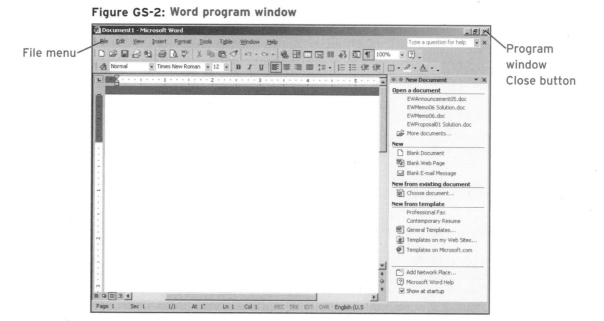

Program window
Close button

Getting Started

Getting Started with Word 2002

Understand Toolbars

Toolbars contain buttons that provide one-click access to frequently used commands. When you start Word, usually only the Standard and Formatting toolbars are visible. Word provides 30 toolbars that contain buttons grouped by specific tasks. For example, the Tables and Borders toolbar contains buttons that you click when you are working with a table in a document. Toolbars are either **docked** along a screen edge, or they are **floating** in the middle of the screen.

Activity Steps

1. Start Word

2. If the Standard and Formatting toolbars are on one line, as shown in Figure GS-3, click either **Toolbar Options button** , then click **Show Buttons on Two Rows**
   The figures in this book show the Standard and Formatting toolbars on two lines.

3. Click **Tools** on the menu bar, click **Customize** to open the Customize dialog box, then click the **Options tab**, if necessary

4. Make sure that the **Show Standard and Formatting toolbars on two rows** check box is selected, then click the **Always show full menus check box** to select it, if necessary

5. Click **Close** in the Customize dialog box

6. Right-click any toolbar, then click **Tables and Borders** to open the Tables and Borders toolbar
   See Figure GS-4.

7. If the Tables and Borders toolbar is not floating as shown in Figure GS-4, position the pointer over a blank area on the toolbar (not over a button), press and hold the mouse button so that the pointer changes to $+$, then drag the toolbar down into a blank area of the window and release the mouse button

8. Click the **Close button** ⊠ in the Tables and Borders toolbar title bar, then exit Word

tip

If you keep the Standard and Formatting toolbars on one line, the button you want may not be visible, so click the Toolbar Options button on either toolbar, then click the button you need.

---

extra!

Using toggle buttons
Toggle means to turn something on or off. Toggle buttons are buttons that are either active (selected) or inactive (deselected). For example, the Drawing button on the Standard toolbar is a toggle button. Clicking it causes the Drawing toolbar to open (usually at the bottom of the window). A blue, square outline appears around an active button, and the button background changes from gray to a light blue. When you click the Drawing button again, the toolbar closes and the button is no longer selected.

Figure GS-3: Word program window with Standard and Formatting toolbars on one line

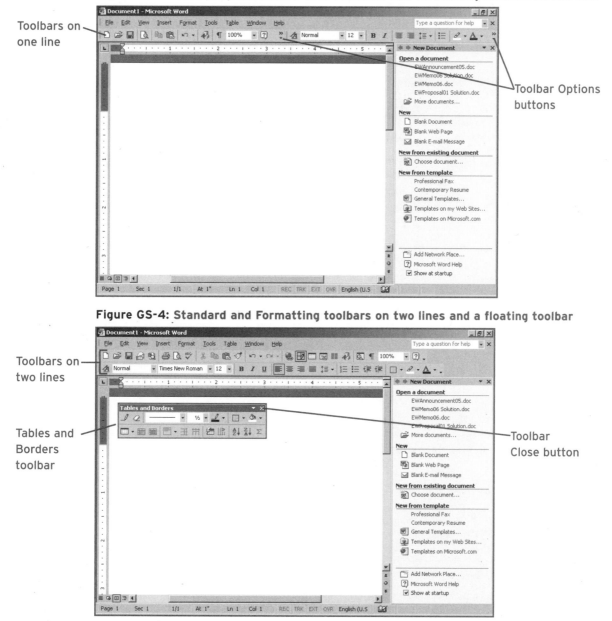

Toolbars on one line

Toolbar Options buttons

Figure GS-4: Standard and Formatting toolbars on two lines and a floating toolbar

Toolbars on two lines

Tables and Borders toolbar

Toolbar Close button

Understand Task Panes

Task panes provide lists of hyperlinks (links) to commonly used commands. They usually appear on the right side of the document window. When you move the pointer over a hyperlink in a taskpane, the pointer changes to 🖑 and the link becomes underlined (similar to links in your browser window). Clicking a link has the same effect as executing a command using the menus or toolbars. Word provides eight task panes (see Table GS-1).

Activity Steps

1. Start Word

2. If a task pane is not open, click **View** on the menu bar, then click **Task Pane**

3. Click the **Other Task Panes list arrow** 🔽 in the task pane title bar, then click **Reveal Formatting** to open the Reveal Formatting task pane

4. Move the pointer over the **Font link** to see the pointer change to 🖑
   See Figure GS-5.

5. Move the pointer over the **Sample Text box** at the top of the task pane to see the list arrow appear

6. Click the **Back button** 🔲 in the task pane title bar to return to the previously displayed task pane

7. Click the **Close button** 🗵 in the task pane title bar to close the task pane
   See Figure GS-6.

8. Exit Word

tip

Right-click any toolbar, then click Task Pane to open or close task panes.

TABLE GS-1: Task panes in Word

task pane	description
New Document	Contains commands for opening new and existing documents
Clipboard	Opens the Office Clipboard, a special area for holding text and objects that you want to paste into the document
Search	Contains commands and options for searching for files that meet specific criteria
Insert Clip Art	Contains commands for searching for clip art (saved images) that meet specific criteria
Styles and Formatting	Contains lists of Word styles (pre-defined formats for text)
Reveal Formatting	Displays a description of the formatting in the selected text
Mail Merge	A set of six panes that helps you merge names and addresses with a form letter
Translate	Contains commands for translating selected text or the entire document to and from French or Spanish

Figure GS-5: Reveal Formatting task pane open

Back button —

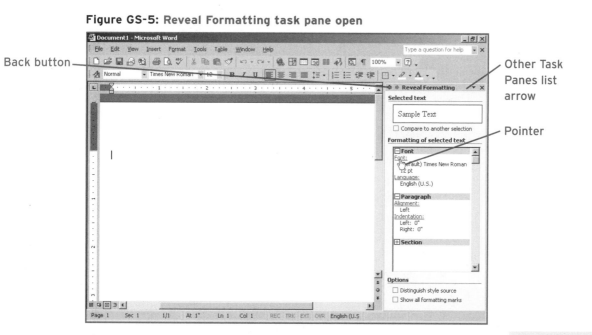

Other Task Panes list arrow

Pointer

Figure GS-6: Document window with no task pane open

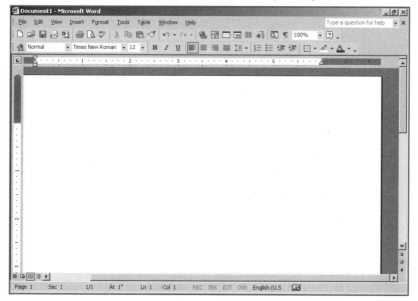

extra!

Using task panes versus using menus and toolbars

Some task pane commands are available on menus or toolbars; for example, you can click the New button to open a new, blank document, or you can click the Blank Document link on the New Document task pane. Other commands are available only on task panes; for example, when you click Search on the File menu, a Search task pane opens, because that is the only place you can enter your search criteria.

Open and Close Documents

In Word, you can create new, blank documents and you can open existing documents to edit them. When you open documents, you can click the list arrow next to the Open command in the Open dialog box to choose one of a variety of ways to open the document (see Table GS-2). When you have finished working on a document, you should close it. It's a good idea to close all open documents before exiting Word.

Activity Steps

1. Start Word, make sure the New Document task pane is open, then click the **Blank Document link** under **New** in the task pane as shown in Figure GS-7 to open another new, blank document

2. Click the **Close Window button** ☒ in the menu bar to close the document

3. Click the **Open button** 🖼 to open the Open dialog box

4. Click the **Look in list arrow**, then select the drive or folder where your project files are stored

5. If your project files are stored within another folder, double-click that folder in the list to display its contents

6. Click the **CCAnnouncement01** file to select it
   See Figure GS-8.

7. Click **Open** to open the selected file

8. Click **File** on the menu bar, then click **Close** to close the document

   Note: In the rest of the book, we assume that you will have Word running or that you will start Word before completing the steps, and that you will exit Word when you have finished.

   When you need to open a file to complete a set of steps, the complete filename will appear next to 🖼 before Step 1. 🖼 will appear again at the end of the steps to remind you to close the file or files you worked on in the skill.

Click the New Blank Document button to open a new, blank document; click the More documents link in the New Document task pane to open the Open dialog box.

Figure GS-7: Closing a document

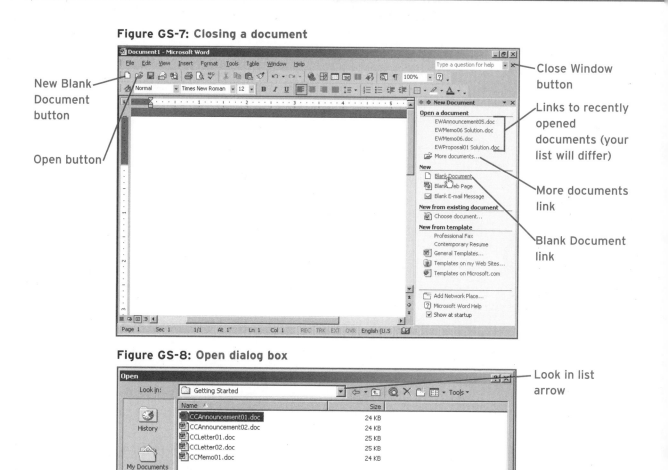

New Blank Document button

Open button

Close Window button

Links to recently opened documents (your list will differ)

More documents link

Blank Document link

Figure GS-8: Open dialog box

Look in list arrow

Open command list arrow

Getting Started

Getting Started with Word 2002

Work with More Than One Open Document

You can open more than one document at a time in Word. The **active document** is the document that you are currently working on. The other documents are **inactive**. You can switch between open documents by clicking the document button on the Windows task bar; by clicking Window on the menu bar, then clicking the document name; or by displaying all of the open document windows on the screen at once and clicking in the one you want to make active.

Activity Steps

open CCAnnouncement01.doc

1. Make sure that Word is running, then make sure you opened the **CCAnnouncement01** file as indicated above

2. Click the **Open button** 📄, navigate to the drive and folder where your project files are stored, click the **CCMemo01** file, then click **Open** to open a second document

3. Click **Window** on the menu bar, then click **CCAnnouncement01**, as shown in Figure GS-9, to make it the active document

4. Click **Window** on the menu bar, then click **Arrange All** to display both documents at the same time
   See Figure GS-10.

5. Click in the **CCMemo01 document window** to make it the active document

6. Press and hold **[Shift]**, click **File** on the menu bar in the CCMemo01 document window, then click **Close All**

7. Click the **Maximize button** ▢ in the Word program window

Step 3
You can also click the document button on the taskbar to switch to another document.

Figure GS-9: Switching between documents using the Windows menu

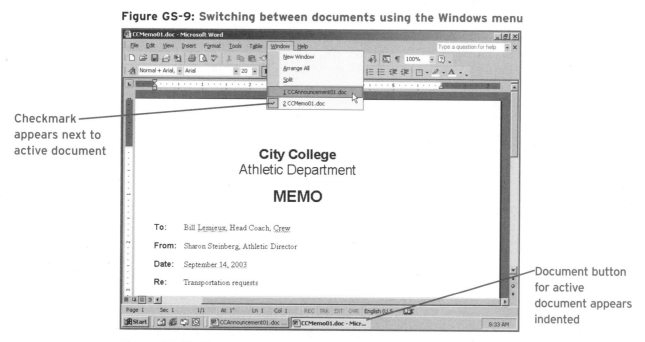

Checkmark appears next to active document

Document button for active document appears indented

Figure GS-10: Two open documents displayed on screen at the same time

Title bar of active document is blue

Title bar of inactive document is gray

Getting Started

Navigate in the Document Window

One of the benefits of working with Word is how easy it is to move around and edit different parts of the document. You can click anywhere in the document to position the **insertion point**, the blinking vertical line that indicates where the text you type will appear. You can also use the keyboard to move the insertion point around in the document (see Table GS-3). Some keys need to be used together to move the insertion point. When you see two keys listed next to each other, such as [Ctrl][Home], you must press and hold the first key, in this case, the [Ctrl] key, then press the second key, in this case, the [Home] key, and then release both keys.

The horizontal scroll bar works the same way as the vertical scroll bar except the document moves sideways in the window.

Activity Steps

 open CCLetter01.doc

1. Make sure that you opened the **CCLetter01** file as indicated above, then click immediately before **crew** in the first line of the body of the letter to position the blinking insertion point there *See Figure GS-11.*

2. Press [➡] five times to move the insertion point to the word **program** in the next line

3. Press **[Page Down]** to move the insertion point down a screen

4. Drag the scroll box in the vertical scroll bar down to the bottom of the scroll bar to see the end of the document without moving the insertion point

5. Click above the scroll box in the vertical scroll bar to jump up a screen

6. Click the down scroll arrow in the vertical scroll bar to scroll down one line

7. Press **[Ctrl][Home]** to move the insertion point to the beginning of the document

8. Make sure you close the **CCLetter01** document as indicated below

 close CCLetter01.doc

Figure GS-11: Insertion point in document

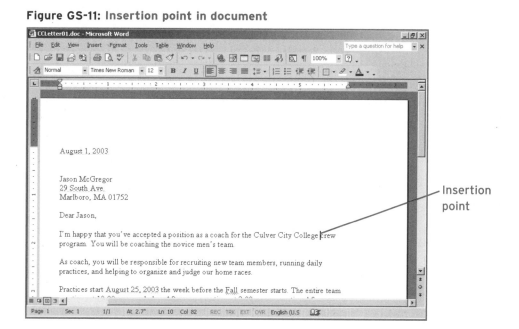

Insertion point

TABLE GS-2: Shortcut keys for moving the insertion point

key	effect
[→], [←]	Moves the insertion point to the right or left one character at a time
[Ctrl][→], [Ctrl][←]	Moves the insertion point to the right or left one word at a time
[↓], [↑]	Moves the insertion point down or up one line
[Page Down], [Page Up]	Moves the insertion point down or up one screen at a time
[Ctrl][Home]	Moves the insertion point to the beginning of the document
[Ctrl][End]	Moves the insertion point to the end of the document
[Home]	Moves the insertion point to the beginning of the current line
[End]	Moves the insertion point to the end of the current line

Getting Started

Getting Started with Word 2002

Understand Views

Word allows you to look at your document in different ways called **views** (see Table GS-3). The default view is Print Layout view. To change the view, you click one of the view buttons located to the left of the horizontal scroll bar. You can also change the **zoom**, the magnification of the document on screen, by clicking the Zoom button list arrow , then selecting another zoom setting from the list, or by clicking in the Zoom box, then typing a new magnification. Changing the view or zoom does not affect how the document will look when printed.

Activity Steps

 open CCAnnouncement02.doc

1. Make sure that you open the **CCAnnouncement02** file as indicated above, then click the **Normal View button** 📄 *See Figure GS-12.*

2. Click the **Web Layout View button** 🖾

3. Click the **Outline View button** 📰

4. Click the **Print Layout View button** 🗎

5. Click the **Zoom button list arrow** `100% ▾`, then click **Whole Page** *See Figure GS-13.*

6. Click in the **Zoom box**, type **60**, then press **[Enter]**

7. Click the **Zoom button list arrow** `60% ▾`, then click **100%**

8. Make sure that you close the **CCAnnouncement02** document as indicated below

 close CCAnnouncement02.doc

You can also change views by selecting a view on the View menu.

TABLE GS-3: Document views

view	what you see
Print Layout view	All of the text, any graphical elements, and headers and footers as they appear on the printed page
Normal view	Formatted text, but not some graphical elements or headers and footers; does not show the document as it will look when printed
Web Layout view	Document as it would look if you published it to a Web page
Outline view	Headings indented to show the structure of the document

Skill 7

Understand Views

Figure GS-12: Document in Normal view

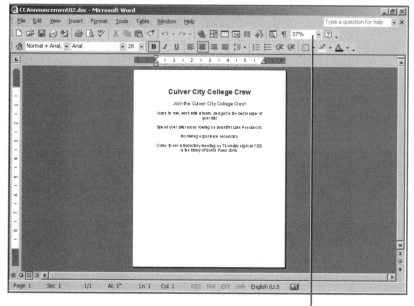

View buttons

Figure GS-13: Document at Whole Page zoom in Print Layout view

Zoom box

extra!

Splitting a document window into two parts

When you work with a long document, it can sometimes be helpful to split the document window into two panes, allowing you to jump back and forth quickly between two parts of the document. The easiest way to do this is to position the pointer on top of the thin split box, just above the up scroll arrow in the vertical scroll bar, so that the pointer changes to ⇌. Drag the split box down to create two panes in the document window. To close the second window, double-click the split box.

Getting Started

Getting Started with Word 2002

Save the Files You Create

As you work through the activities in this book, you might want to save your completed files. You will learn more about saving files in Skill Set 4, but in the meantime, you can save your files in one of two ways. If you want to leave the original files that you open unchanged, you can save your completed files with a new name by using the Save As command on the File menu. If you don't care if the original file changes, you can save the changes that you make when you complete the steps to the same file that you opened by clicking the Save button .

Activity Steps

file> open CCMemo01.doc

1. Make sure that you opened the **CCMemo01** file as indicated above, click **File** on the menu bar, then click **Save As** to open the Save As dialog box

2. Click the **Save in list arrow**, then select the drive or folder where you want to store your files

3. If you are storing your files within another folder, double-click that folder in the list to display its contents

4. Select the text in the **File name box** if it's not already selected, then type **Intro Letter** in the Filename box
   See Figure GS-14.

5. Click **Save** to save the document with the new name and leave the original document unchanged

6. Type **Culver**, then press the **[Spacebar]**

7. Click the **Save button** to save the changes to the document with the same filename
   See Figure GS-15.

8. Make sure that you close the **Intro letter** document as indicated below

file> close Intro Letter.doc

> **tip**
>
> Copy all of the project files before you use them to complete the skills in this book. This will allow you to repeat the steps for any skills that you want to review.

---

extra!

Closing without saving
If you do not want to save the changes you made to the documents as you work through the activities, you can simply close the files without saving them first. When you do this, a warning box will appear asking if you want to save the changes to the file. If you click No, the file closes without saving your changes. If you click Yes, the changes you made are saved, then the file closes.

Figure GS-14: Save As dialog box

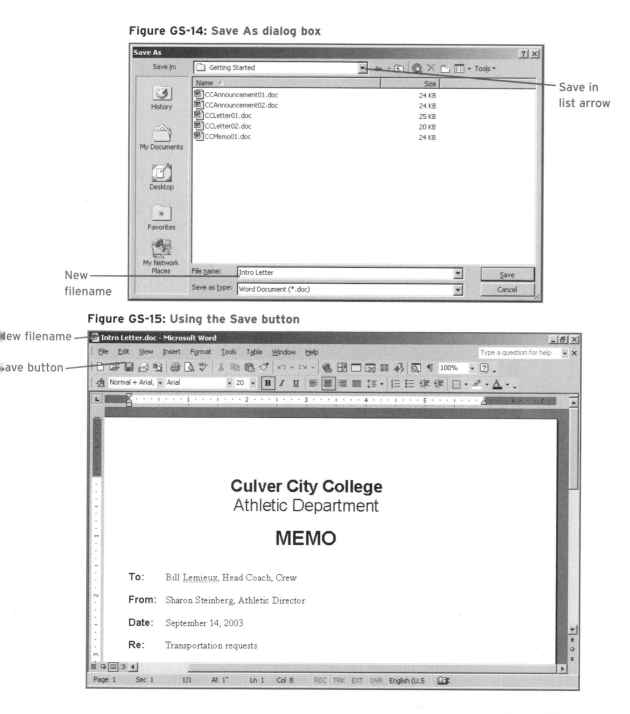

Save in list arrow

New filename

New filename

Save button

Figure GS-15: Using the Save button

Getting Started

Getting Started with Word 2002

Use Smart Tags

A **smart tag** is a button that appears on screen when Word recognizes a word or phrase as belonging to a certain category, for example, names, addresses, and dates. When you click the button, you can choose to add the name or address to your electronic address book, or you can choose to add the date to your electronic scheduler. Some smart tags do not appear until you position the pointer over their locations, which are identified by a dotted red line under a word or phrase.

Step 4

If the Outlook 2002 startup wizard screen appears, you will need to use it to set up Outlook before you can complete Steps 4 and 5. Follow the wizard steps, or click Cancel in the wizard, then continue with Step 6.

Activity Steps

 open CCLetter02.doc

1. Make sure that you opened the **CCLetter02** file as indicated above, then move the pointer over the **date** in the first line to see the smart tag  appear
See Figure GS-16.

2. Point to the **smart tag** to make the Smart Tag Actions button appear

3. Click the **Smart Tag Actions button** to open the drop-down list
See Figure GS-17.

4. Click **Schedule a Meeting** on the drop-down list to open your electronic calendar

5. Click the **Close button** in the calendar program window, then click **No** when asked if you want to save changes

6. Move the pointer over the **street address** in the inside address to display the smart tag, move the pointer over the **smart tag**, then click the **Smart Tag Actions button**

7. Click **Remove this Smart Tag**

8. Make sure that you close the **CCLetter02** document as indicated below, clicking **No** when asked if you want to save changes

close CCLetter02.doc

---

extra!

Changing smart tag options
You can change what type of text is labeled by Word with smart tags. Click Smart Tag Options on the Smart Tag Actions button drop down list, or click AutoCorrect Options on the Tools menu, then click the Smart Tags tab. Click the check boxes in the Recognizers list to select or deselect the types of text you want to be recognized. If you are connected to the World Wide Web, you can also click More Smart Tags on the Smart Tags tab in the AutoCorrect Options dialog box. This will connect you to a Microsoft Web site, where you can find more Smart Tags you can download.

Figure GS-16: Displaying a smart tag

Smart tag

Pointer

Red dotted
line identifies
the location of
a smart tag

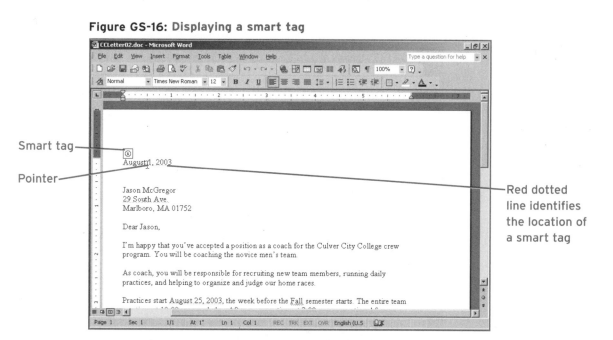

Figure GS-17: Using the Smart Tag Actions button

Smart Tag
Actions
button

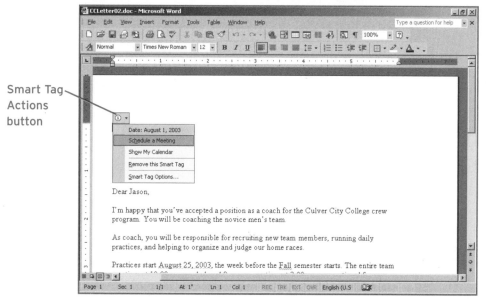

Getting Started

Getting Started with Word 2002

Get Help

Word provides an online Help system to help you find information about Word and instructions on how to use Word commands and features. The easiest way to access the Help system is to type a question in the Ask a Question box in the menu bar in the program window. You can also open the Help window by pressing [F1] or by clicking the Microsoft Word Help button 📝 .

Step 6
If the topics shown in Figure GS-19 do not appear on your screen, click the plus sign next to Microsoft Word Help in the Contents tab, then click the plus sign next to Viewing and Navigating Documents.

Activity Steps

1. Click in the **Ask a Question box** `Type a question for help` in the menu bar

2. Type **Look at two parts of a document**, then press **[Enter]**
   See Figure GS-18.

3. Click the **See more link** at the bottom of the drop-down list

4. Click the **View two parts of a document simultaneously link** to open a Help window displaying this information

5. If the Help window is not expanded as shown in Figure GS-19, click the **Show button** 🔲 in the Help window toolbar to expand the Help window

6. Click the **Contents tab** in the pane on the left of the Help window, if necessary, then click **Move around in a document** as shown in Figure GS-19

7. Click the **plus sign** next to **Getting Started with Microsoft Word** in the Contents tab to expand that topic list

8. Click the **Back button** ⬅ at the top of the Help window to return to the previous Help screen, then click the **Close button** ✖ in the Help window title bar to close the Help window

Skill 10

Get Help

Figure GS-18: Selecting a Help topic from the Ask a Question box drop-down list

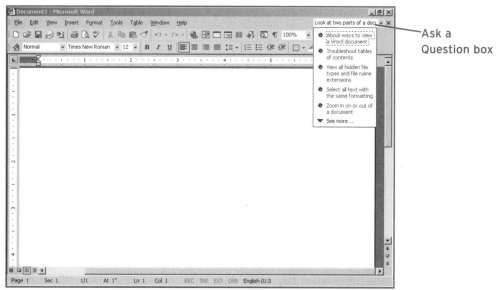

Ask a
Question box

Figure GS-19: Contents tab in the Help window

Click plus sign to
expand topic list

Click minus sign
to collapse topic
list

Click this topic
to display new
information in
pane on the right

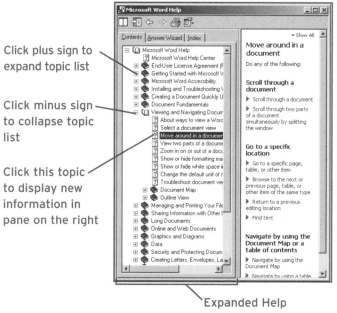

Expanded Help
window

Target Your Skills

Target Your Skills

If you know the answers to the following questions, then you are ready to move ahead to the rest of the chapters in this book. If you have trouble with any of the questions, refer to the page listed next to the question to review the skill.

1. How do you start Word? How do you exit Word? (p. 2)

2. What is the three-letter filename extension for Word documents? Name two other filename extensions that Word recognizes. (p. 3)

3. Describe a toolbar. How are toolbars positioned in the window? Describe two ways to close a toolbar. (p. 4)

4. Define **toggle**. (p. 5)

5. Describe task panes. How do you open a task pane? Describe three ways to close a task pane. (p. 6)

6. How do you open a new, blank document? How do you open an existing document? Describe two ways to close a document. (p. 8)

7. Define **active document**. Describe two ways to switch between open documents. Explain how to display two open documents on the screen at the same time. (p. 10)

8. to the beginning of a document? (p. 12)

9. Describe the four views in Word. Explain what the Zoom command does. (p. 14)

10. How do you split a document window in two? (p. 15)

11. How do you save changes to a document? How do you save a document with a new name? How do you save a new document for the first time? (p. 16)

12. Can you close a document without saving changes that you made? (p. 17)

13. Define **smart tag**. How are smart tags identified in a document? (p. 18)

14. How do you access Word's online Help system? (p. 20)

Skill List

1. Insert, modify, and move text and symbols
2. Apply and modify text formats
3. Correct spelling and grammar usage
4. Apply font and text effects
5. Enter and format date and time
6. Apply character styles

In Skill Set 1, you will learn how to create a document in Microsoft Word 2002. A **document** is any file that you create using Word. You can create many kinds of documents, including memos, letters, newsletters, resumes, brochures, and multi-page reports.

Once you insert text into a document, you can modify that text in several ways. You can change the words or the word order. If you want, you can change the way the text looks by modifying the format of the text. You can also use Word to check your spelling and grammar and to automatically insert the current date and time.

Skill Set 1

Inserting and Modifying Text

Insert, Modify, and Move Text and Symbols
Insert Text

The first thing you do when you create a document is insert text. To do this, you simply start typing using the keyboard. The blinking **insertion point** on the screen indicates where the text will appear. When you reach the end of a line, the insertion point automatically moves to the next line—you do not need to press [Enter]. This is called **word-wrap**. You press [Enter] when you want to start a new paragraph. To add a blank line between paragraphs, you can press [Enter] twice.

You do not need to type two spaces after any punctuation, because Word adjusts the space automatically.

Activity Steps

1. Create a new, blank document
2. Type **November 3, 2003**, then press **[Enter]** twice
   See Figure 1-1.
3. Type **Ms. Patsy Madison**, then press **[Enter]**
4. Type **503 Shore Drive**, then press **[Enter]**
5. Type **Charleston, SC 29407**, then press **[Enter]** twice
6. Type **Dear Ms. Madison:**, then press **[Enter]** twice
7. Type the body of the letter shown in Figure 1-2, then press **[Enter]** twice at the end of the paragraph
8. Type **Sincerely**, press **[Enter]** four times, then type your name

 close file

Figure 1-1: Text entered in a new document

Insertion point ——

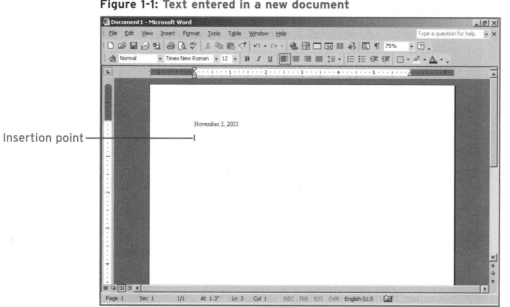

Figure 1-2: Document with paragraphs

Your text may
wrap at a
different point

Replace with
your name

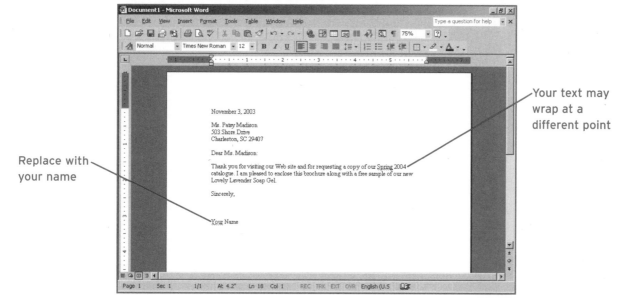

Skill Set 1

Inserting and Modifying Text

Insert, Modify, and Move Text and Symbols
Insert Symbols

In addition to letters and numbers, you can enter symbols in a document. A **symbol** is a character not included in the standard English alphabet or set of Arabic numbers. You enter symbols using the Symbol dialog box.

Click the Special
Characters tab in
the Symbol dialog
box to see a short
list of common
symbols.

Activity Steps

 open EWLetter01.doc

1. Click ⌶ immediately after the word **Soap** in the third line, so that the insertion point blinks to the left of the period

2. Click **Insert** on the menu bar, then click **Symbol** to open the Symbol dialog box

3. Click the **Font list arrow**, then click to select **Times New Roman**, if necessary

4. Drag the **scroll box** to the top of the scroll bar, then click the **down scroll arrow** three times

5. Click ©, the copyright symbol
   See Figure 1-3.

6. Click **Insert**, then click **Close**
   See Figure 1-4.

 close EWLetter01.doc

Figure 1-3: Symbol dialog box

Copyright symbol

Description of selected symbol

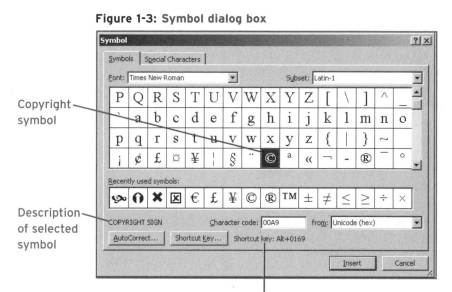

Shortcut key combination
to insert selected symbol

Figure 1-4: Symbol inserted in document

Copyright symbol inserted

Skill Set 1
Inserting and Modifying Text

Insert, Modify, and Move Text and Symbols
Edit Text

With a word processor, you do not need to retype an entire document when you want to change a word or delete a sentence. The easiest way to edit text is to use the [Backspace] and [Delete] keys. When you press [Backspace], you delete the character immediately to the left of the insertion point. When you press [Delete], you delete the character immediately to the right of the insertion point. You can also **select**, or highlight, the text you want to change and then start typing, and the characters you type will replace all of the selected text.

If you make a mistake, you can "undo" it by clicking the Undo button. Undo any number of previous actions by clicking the list arrow next to the Undo button, then selecting as many actions as you want.

Activity Steps

 open EWMemo01.doc

1. Click immediately to the right of **Seaview** in the first paragraph in the body of the memo

2. Press **[Backspace]** seven times, then type **Riverside**

3. Click immediately to the left of **20** (after **June**) in the first paragraph

4. Press **[Delete]** twice, then type **19**

5. Double-click the word **three** in the first line in the first paragraph to select it

6. Type **four**
   See Figure 1-5.

 close EWMemo01.doc

Figure 1-5: Document with edited text

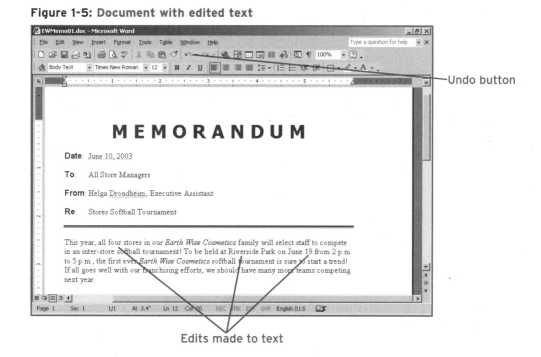

Undo button

Edits made to text

extra!

Selecting text

There are several ways to select text. You can position the pointer to one side of the text you want to select, press and hold the mouse button, drag the pointer across the text to select it, then release the mouse button. To select a word quickly, double-click it. To select a line of text, position the pointer in the blank area on the left side of the document to the left of the line, so that the pointer changes to ⇗, then click. To select a large body of text, click at the beginning of the text you want to select, press and hold [Shift], then click at the end of the text. You can also use the keyboard to select text. Position the pointer to the left or right of the text you want to select, press and hold [Shift], then press [➡] or [⬅] as many times as necessary to select the word or phrase. To select a word at a time, press and hold [Shift] and [Ctrl] while you press [➡] or [⬅].

Skill Set 1
Inserting and Modifying Text

Insert, Modify, and Move Text and Symbols
Cut and Paste Text

You use the Cut and Paste commands to move text from one place in a document to another, or even from one document to another. When you **cut** text, it is removed from the document and stored in the system **clipboard**. When you **paste** text, you are pasting whatever is stored on the clipboard. You can paste the text you stored on the clipboard as many times as you like. The system clipboard can hold only one thing at a time, so each time you cut text, you replace whatever was stored there before. The clipboard is cleared when you shut off your computer.

Activity Steps

 open EWLetter02.doc

1. Double-click the word **online** in the first sentence of the second paragraph within the body of the letter
2. Click the **Cut button**
3. Click between the words **completed** and **that** in the second paragraph
4. Click the **Paste button**
5. Scroll down until you can see the third paragraph
6. Click to position the insertion point before the word **Again** in the third paragraph, press and hold the mouse button, drag to highlight the entire first sentence including the space after the period, then release the mouse button
7. Point to the selected sentence and hold down the mouse button
8. Drag down so that the vertical indicator line attached to the pointer appears after the last sentence in the paragraph
   See Figure 1-6.
9. Release the mouse button to position the dragged sentence at the end of the paragraph
   See Figure 1-7.

 close EWLetter02.doc

Click the Paste Options button that appears on the screen after you perform the Paste command or drag and drop text to choose options for changing the format of the pasted text.

---

extra!

Understanding the Office Clipboard
With Office XP you can use the standard system clipboard or the Office Clipboard. The system clipboard can store only the most recently cut or copied item. The Office Clipboard which opens as a task pane, can store up to 24 items. To activate it, click Office Clipboard on the Edit menu or perform several cut, copy, and paste commands in succession. To paste an item from the Office Clipboard, click the item in the Clipboard task pane. (When you use the Paste command, you paste only the last item placed on the system clipboard.)

Figure 1-6: Document with moved text and sentence being dragged and dropped

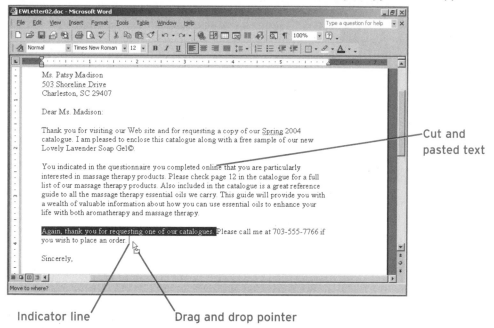

Cut and pasted text

Indicator line

Drag and drop pointer

Figure 1-7: Document after sentence is dropped in new location

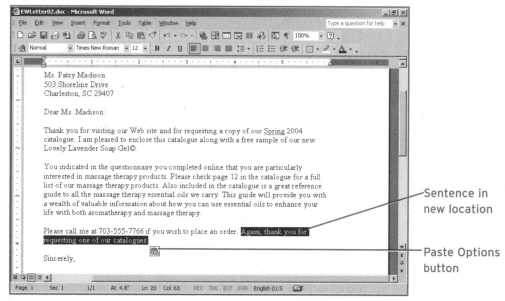

Sentence in new location

Paste Options button

Skill Set 1

Inserting and Modifying Text

Insert, Modify, and Move Text and Symbols
Copy and Paste Text

Copying is similar to cutting, but when you copy text, you don't remove it from its original location. As with cutting, whatever you copy is placed on the clipboard for you to paste as many times as you want, until you replace it with new cut or copied text.

Right-click selected text, then click Cut or Copy. Right-click where you want to paste the text, then click Paste.

Activity Steps

 open EWLetter03.doc

1. Select **Mr. Ng** in the salutation (do not select the colon)

2. Click the **Copy button**

3. Click immediately after **thank you** in the first line in the last paragraph, type , (a comma), then press the **[Spacebar]**

4. Click the **Paste button** , then type , (a comma)
   See Figure 1-8.

5. Double-click **catalogue** in the second line in the first paragraph

6. Press and hold **[Ctrl]**, then drag **catalogue** between **the** and **for** in the second line in the second paragraph
   See Figure 1-9.

close EWLetter03.doc

Figure 1-8: Text copied to new location

Copied text

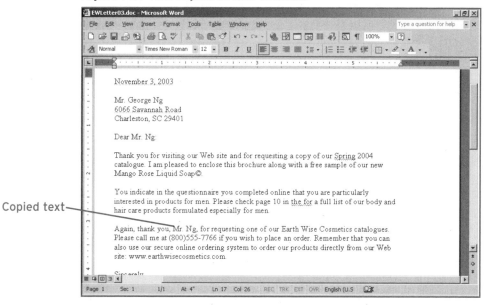

Figure 1-9: Copied text being dragged and dropped

Indicator line

Drag and drop copy pointer

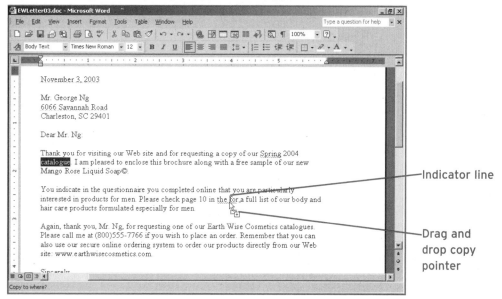

Skill Set 1
Inserting and Modifying Text

Insert, Modify, and Move Text and Symbols
Use the Paste Special Command

The Paste Special command allows you to control how information is pasted by giving you a variety of paste options. You can use it when you cut or copy something from one place in a Word document to another place in the same document, when you cut or copy between Word documents, or when you cut or copy from a file created in another program to a Word document. You can also use it to copy formatted text—text with a specific appearance—to another paragraph that is formatted differently, and have the pasted text pick up the formatting of its destination paragraph.

Another way to paste copied text so that it picks up the formatting of the destination paragraph is to use the Paste command, click the Paste Options button that appears on screen, then click Match Destination Formatting.

Activity Steps

file
 open EWBrochure01.doc
   EWLetter04.doc

1. Click **Window** on the menu bar, then click **EWBrochure01.doc**

2. Select the entire paragraph under the heading **Lavender Soap Gel** (do not select the heading or the blank line below the paragraph)
See Figure 1-10.

3. Click the **Copy button**

4. Click **Window** on the menu bar, then click **EWLetter04.doc**

5. Click at the end of the first paragraph, after the period

6. Click **Edit** on the menu bar, click **Paste Special**, then click **Unformatted Text** in the list in the Paste Special dialog box

7. Click **OK** to paste the copied text so it picks up the formatting of the destination paragraph
See Figure 1-11.

file
 close EWBrochure01.doc
   EWLetter04.doc

Figure 1-10: Formatted text selected in a document

EWBrochure01
is the active file

Selected text

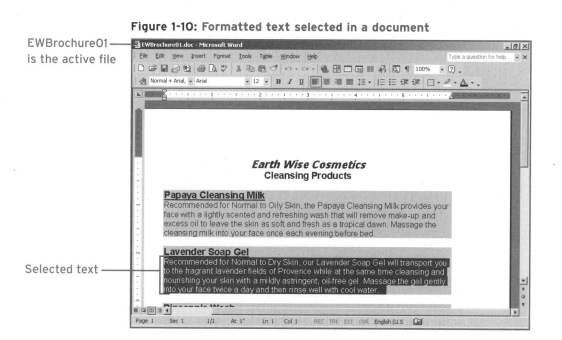

Figure 1-11: Pasted text with the formatting of the destination paragraph

EWLetter04 is
the active file

Inserted text picks
up formatting of
this paragraph

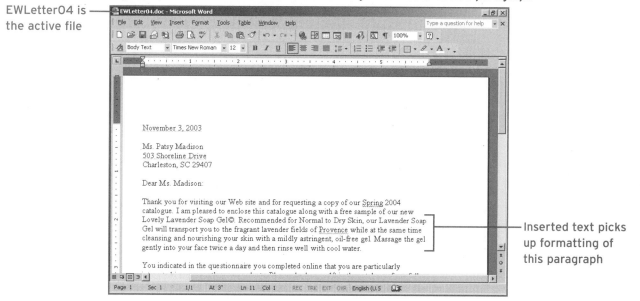

Skill Set 1

Inserting and Modifying Text

Insert, Modify, and Move Text and Symbols
Find and Replace Text

In a long document, you may need to locate a specific word or phrase. You may also want to replace that word or phrase with another. The Find and Replace commands in Word let you do this easily and quickly. Enter the word or words for which you are searching, and then tell Word to find them. If you want to replace the words you find, you can enter the new words and tell Word to replace the search terms.

Activity Steps

 open EWLetter05.doc

1. Click **Edit** on the menu bar, then click **Find** to open the Find and Replace dialog box

2. Type **massage therapy** in the Find what box

3. Click **Find Next**
   See Figure 1-12.

4. Click the **Replace tab** in the Find and Replace dialog box, click in the Replace with box, then type **aromatherapy**

5. Click **Replace** to replace the search term with the replacement term and to find the next instance of the search term in the document

6. Click **Replace** two more times to replace the next two instances of the search term
   See Figure 1-13.

7. Click **Find Next** to skip this instance of the search term and find the next one

8. Click **OK** in the dialog box that appears telling you that Word has finished searching the document, then click **Close** in the Find and Replace dialog box

 close EWLetter05.doc

tip

If you are sure that you want to replace all instances of the text for which you are searching, click Replace All on the Replace tab in the Find and Replace dialog box.

---

extra!

Finding formatted text and special characters
You can search for text with specific formatting as well as special characters. Click More in the Find and Replace dialog box, then click Format or Special. For example, if you wanted to find all the words with bold formatting, click in the Find what box, click Format, click Font, click Bold, then click OK. When you click Find Next, Word searches for words with bold formatting. To remove formatting options from the search criteria, click No Formatting.

Figure 1-12: Using the Find command

Text found in document

Find what box

Figure 1-13: Replacing text

Replaced text

Don't replace this instance

Click to see more options

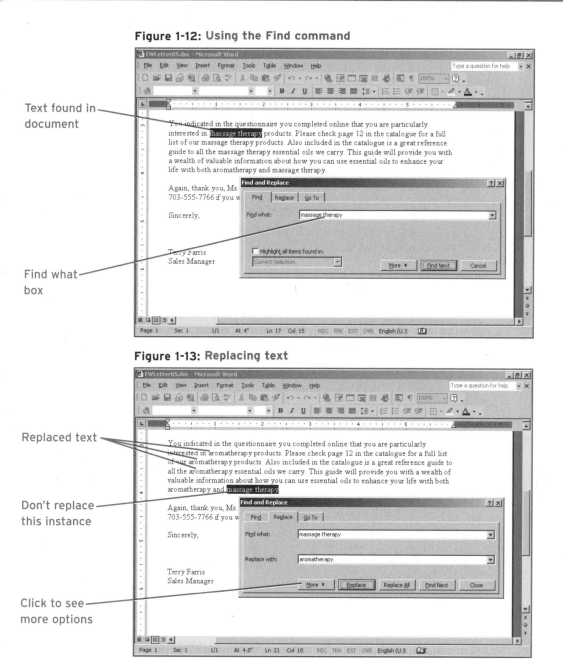

Skill Set 1

Inserting and Modifying Text

Insert, Modify, and Move Text and Symbols
Create AutoText Entries and Use AutoComplete

You can store frequently used words or phrases as AutoText, text that Word automatically enters. When you type the first few characters of an AutoText entry, a ScreenTip appears identifying it as AutoText. You can then use the AutoComplete feature by pressing [Enter] to insert the rest of the word or phrase automatically.

To see the predefined AutoText entries, click Tools on the menu bar, click AutoCorrect Options, then click the AutoText tab and scroll down the list.

Activity Steps

 open EWAnnouncement01.doc

1. Select **Earth Wise Cosmetics** in the first line in the document

2. Click **Insert** on the menu bar, point to **AutoText**, then click **New** to open the Create AutoText dialog box

3. Click **OK** to accept the suggested name for the AutoText entry

4. Click immediately before the word **Softball** in the last paragraph

5. Type **eart** to see the AutoComplete ScreenTip
   See Figure 1-14.

6 Press **[Enter]** to complete the AutoText entry
   See Figure 1-15.

7. Click **Insert** on the menu bar, point to **AutoText**, then click **AutoText** to open the AutoText tab in the AutoCorrect dialog box

8. Type **e** in the Enter AutoText Entries here box to jump to the entries beginning with **e** in the list, click **Earth Wise** in the list, click **Delete**, then click **OK** to close the dialog box

 close EWAnnouncement01.doc

Figure 1-14: AutoComplete ScreenTip

AutoComplete
screen tip

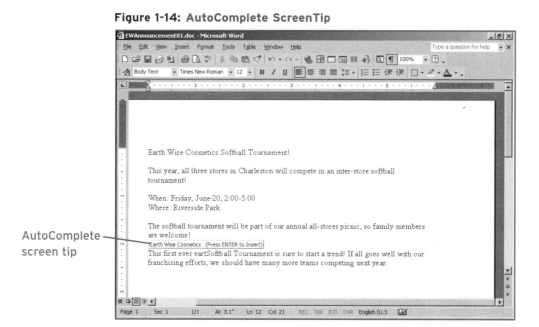

Figure 1-15: Completed AutoText entry in document

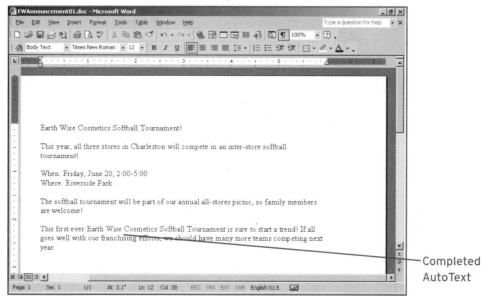

Completed
AutoText

Skill Set 1

Inserting and Modifying Text

Insert, Modify, and Move Text and Symbols

Use AutoCorrect

AutoCorrect automatically detects and corrects frequently misspelled words, and it checks for and corrects incorrect capitalization. It also replaces text with symbols. For example, if you type *teh*, as soon as you press the [Spacebar] or [Enter], AutoCorrect replaces the mistyped word with *the*. You can add your own frequently typed words to the AutoCorrect list to cut down on the number of keystrokes you need to make.

Activity Steps

 open EWBrochure02.doc

1. Click below the **Lavender Soap Gel** heading, then type **We reccommend** with two *c*s exactly as shown

2. Press the **[Spacebar]**, watching the screen as you do to see AutoCorrect correct the spelling of **recommend**

3. Move the pointer over the word **recommend** to see the AutoCorrect Options button ▭
   See Figure 1-16.

To change the types of words automatically corrected, open the AutoCorrect tab in the AutoCorrect dialog box, and deselect any check boxes you wish.

4. Move the pointer over the **AutoCorrect Options button** ▭ to change it to a button icon ▭

5. Click the **AutoCorrect Options button** ▭, click **Control AutoCorrect Options** in the drop-down menu to open the AutoCorrect tab in the AutoCorrect dialog box, scroll down the list to see the AutoCorrect entries, then click **OK**

6. Type **this gle for** and observe the red, squiggly line under **gle** that indicates the word is misspelled

7. Right-click the misspelled word **gle**, point to AutoCorrect on the shortcut menu, then click **gel** as shown in Figure 1-17 to add this misspelling to the AutoCorrect list and correct the word in the document

8. Click **Tools** on the menu bar, click **AutoCorrect Options**, type **gl** in the Replace box to scroll the list, click **gle** in the list, click **Delete**, then click **OK** to delete the word you added from the AutoCorrect list

 close EWBrochure02.doc

Figure 1-16: AutoCorrect box in document

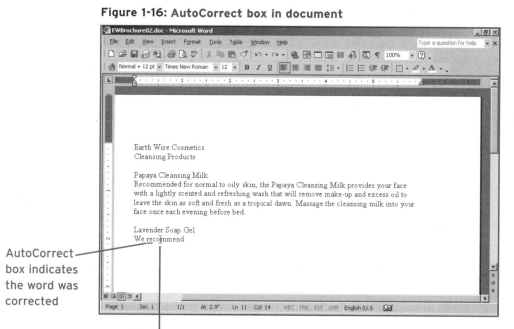

AutoCorrect box indicates the word was corrected

Pointer

Figure 1-17: Adding a word to the AutoCorrect list automatically

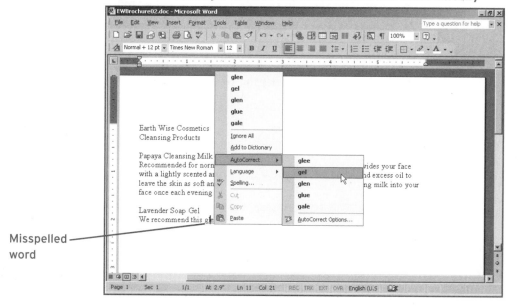

Misspelled word

Skill Set 1
Inserting and Modifying Text

Apply and Modify Text Formats
Apply Character Formats

Format refers to the way something looks. Specifically, you can add formatting to text by changing the **font** (the design of letters and numbers), the **font size**, and the **font style** (for example, adding boldface or italics). Judicious use of text formatting commands can make a document easier to read. Most text formatting can be accomplished using the buttons on the Formatting toolbar.

If unexpected changes occur as you type, click the AutoFormat As You Type tab in the AutoCorrect dialog box, then deselect the check boxes next to the items you want to stop formatting automatically.

Activity Steps

 open EWCoDescription01.doc

1. Select the first line of text, then click the **Bold button** B

2. Click the **Font box list arrow** Times New Roman ▾ , scroll, if necessary, then click **Arial**

3. Click the **Font Size box list arrow** 12 ▾ , click **16**, then click in a blank area of the screen to deselect the text
   See Figure 1-18.

4. Select the second line of text, click the **Bold button** B , click the **Italic button** I , then change the font size to **14**

5. Click the **Bold button** B again to turn bold formatting off for the selected text

6. Select the third line of text, then click the **Underline button** U

7. Repeat step 6 for the **Company Background** line, then click in a blank area of the screen to deselect the text
   See Figure 1-19.

 close EWCoDescription01.doc

extra!

Understanding points and picas
Points and picas are units of measurement for text. A **point** (pt) is approximately 1/72 of an inch, and a **pica** is equivalent to 12 points. Typically, fonts are measured in points, space between paragraphs is measured in points and picas, and margins and paragraph indents are measured in inches.

Figure 1-18: Document after formatting first line of text

Format of
text changed

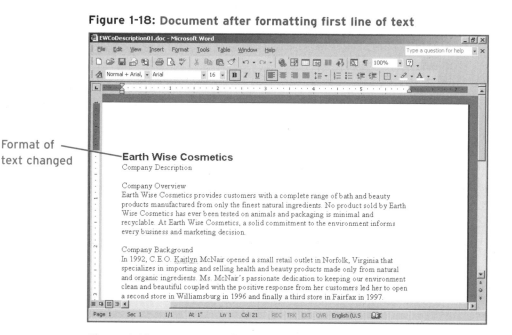

Figure 1-19: Document after formatting headings

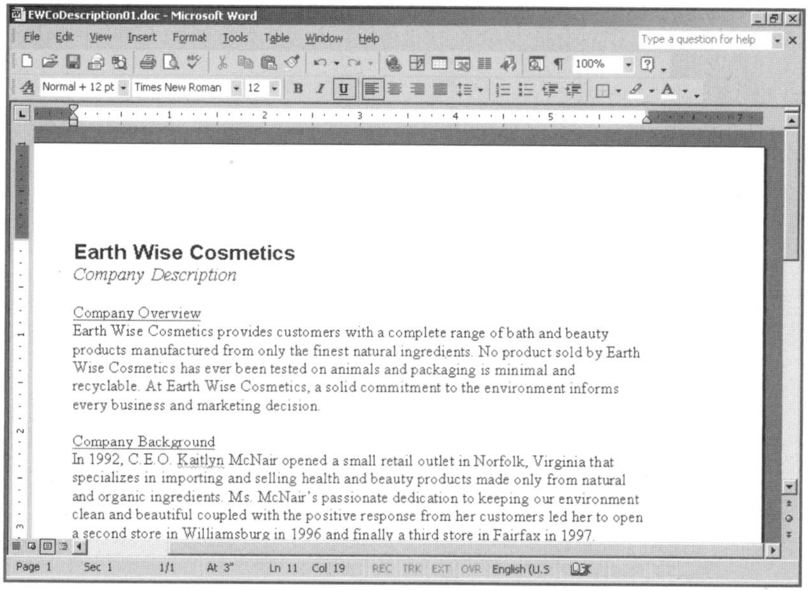

Skill Set 1

Inserting and Modifying Text

Apply and Modify Text Formats
Modify Character Formats

After you have applied formatting to characters, you can change it in any way you wish. Once you have formatted text the way you want, you can copy that formatting to other text in your document by using the Format Painter button.

To format text in different areas of the document with Format Painter, select the text whose format you want to copy, then double-click the Format Painter button. It will remain active until you click it again.

Activity Steps

📁 open EWAnnouncement02.doc

1. Select the first line of text
   See Figure 1-20.

2. Click the **Font size list arrow** 22, then click **18**

3. Click the **Font Color list arrow** ▲▾, then click the **Lavender color box** (last row, second to last column)

4. Select **When:**, click the **Bold button** B to turn the bold formatting off, then click the **Underline button** U

5. With **When:** still selected, click the **Format Painter button** 🖌

6. Drag across **Where:** to select it
   See Figure 1-21.

7. Click in a blank area of the screen to deselect the text

📁 close EWAnnouncement02.doc

Figure 1-20: Formatted text selected

Buttons reflect the formatting of the selected text

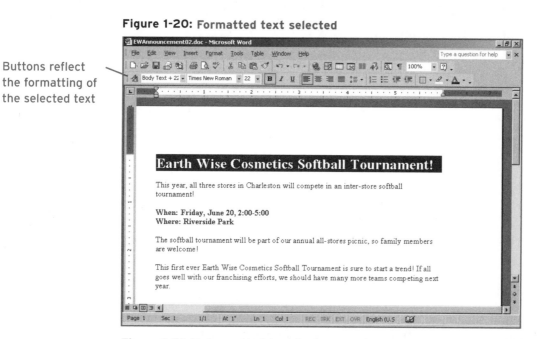

Figure 1-21: Reformatted text in document

Format Painter selected

Pointer

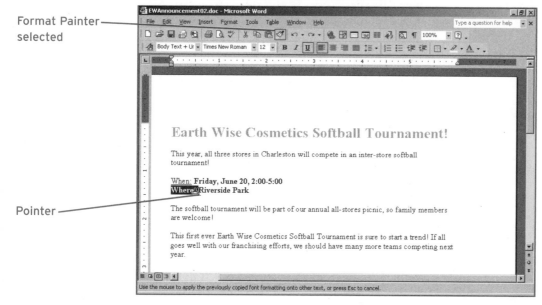

Skill Set 1

Inserting and Modifying Text

Correct Spelling and Grammar Usage
Correct Spelling Errors

When you click the Spelling command, Word scans the document and compares the words against its built-in dictionary. When it finds a word that isn't in its dictionary, it flags it as a possible misspelled word and offers a list of suggested corrections. You can choose one of the corrections from the list, correct the word yourself, or tell Word to ignore the word (in other words, that it is spelled correctly). If automatic spell checking is turned on, you will see red, squiggly lines under the words that Word is flagging as misspelled.

Right-click a word with a red, squiggly underline to open a shortcut menu containing a list of suggested corrections. Click a suggested correction or click Ignore All.

Activity Steps

 open EWLetter06.doc

1. Click the **Spelling and Grammar button**
   See Figure 1-22.

2. Click **catalog** in the Suggestions list, then click **Change All** to change all instances of the flagged word and search for the next possible misspelling

3. Click **Ignore All** to ignore all instances of the word **Provence** (a proper noun) and continue searching

4. Click **Change** to accept the selected entry **twice** in the Suggestions list and continue searching

5. Click **Change** to accept the selected entry **catalogs** in the Suggestions list and continue searching

6. Click **OK** in the dialog box that appears telling you that the spelling and grammar check is complete

 close EWLetter06.doc

Figure 1-22: Spelling dialog box

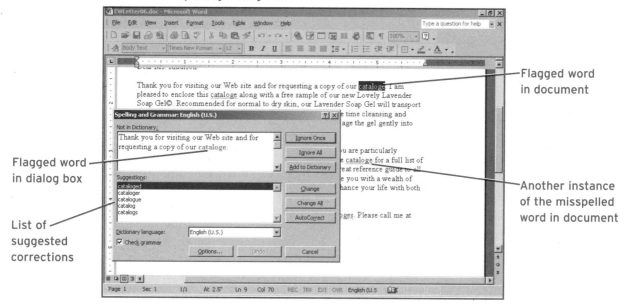

Flagged word in document

Flagged word in dialog box

List of suggested corrections

Another instance of the misspelled word in document

extra!

Changing Spelling and Grammar options

To change Spelling and Grammar checker options, click Options in the Spelling and Grammar dialog box or click Tools on the menu bar, click Options, then click the Spelling & Grammar tab. To hide the red and green squiggly lines in your document, deselect the check boxes next to Check spelling as you type and Check grammar as you type. To check style as well as grammar, click the arrow under Writing style and select Grammar and Style in the list. To change the Grammar checker rules, click Settings, then deselect the check boxes next to the items you don't want to check. If you have already checked the document for spelling and grammar errors but you want to recheck it, click Recheck Document to reset all of the items that you previously had told the Spelling and Grammar checker to ignore.

Skill Set 1
Inserting and Modifying Text

Correct Spelling and Grammar Usage
Correct Grammar Errors

The grammar checker is part of the spell checker. If the Check grammar check box in the Spelling and Grammar dialog box is selected, the grammar in your document will be checked at the same time as the spelling.

Activity Steps

 open EWLetter07.doc

1. Click the **Spelling and Grammar button**
   See Figure 1-23.

2. Click **Explain,** then read the explanation that appears when the Office Assistant appears

3. Click **Ignore Once** to ignore this rule (*Spring* is a title in the document, not a season) and continue the search

4. Click in the document behind the Spelling and Grammar dialog box, position the insertion point immediately after the **e** in **guide** in the highlighted sentence, press the **[Spacebar]**, then type **will**
   See Figure 1-24.

5. Click **Resume** in the Spelling and Grammar dialog box

6. Click the second suggestion in the Suggestions list, then click **Change**

7. Click **OK** in the dialog box that appears telling you that the spelling and grammar check is complete

 close EWLetter07.doc

The grammar checker is not perfect. It compares sentences against a built-in set of rules, but it may miss errors or identify something that is correct as an error, so use your common sense.

Figure 1-23: Grammar problem flagged by Spelling and Grammar checker

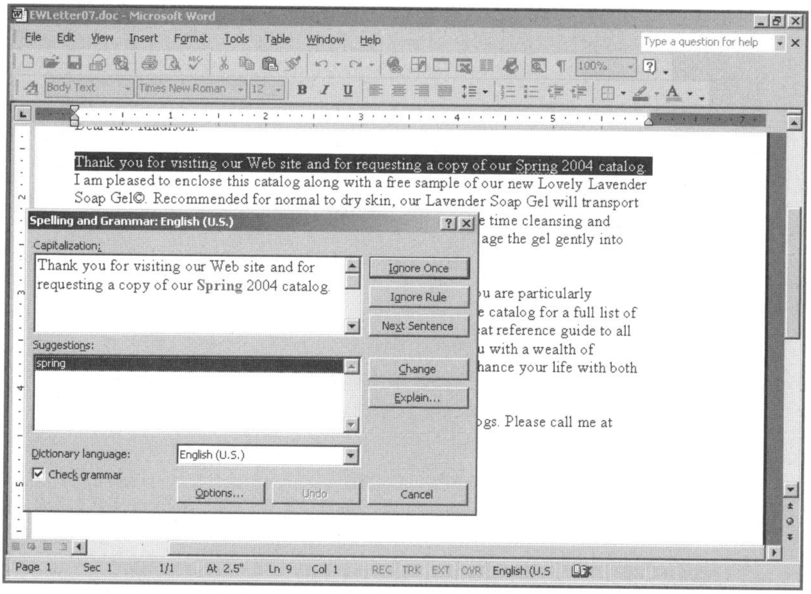

Figure 1-24: Fixing an error in the document

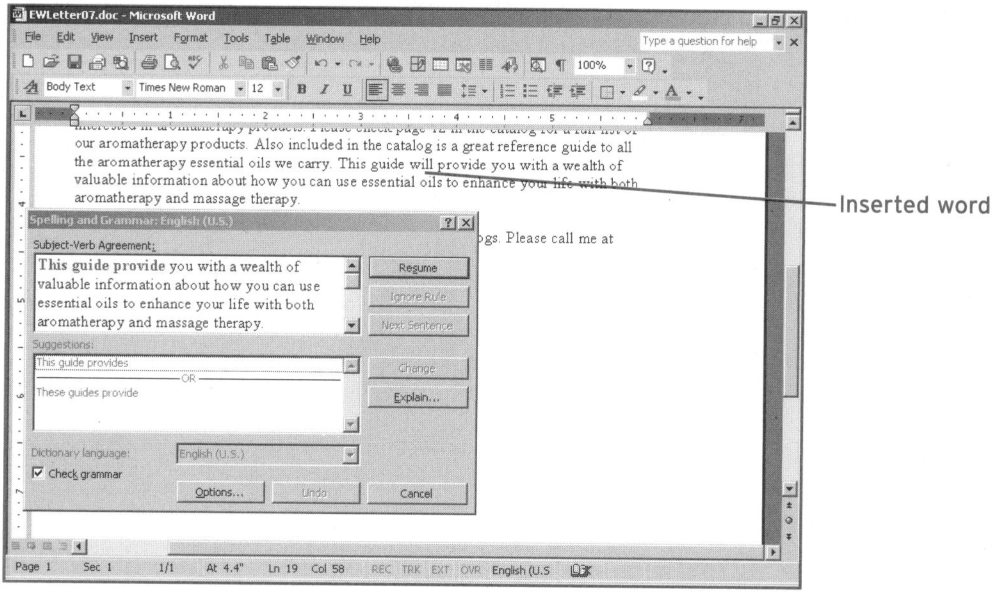

Inserted word

Skill Set 1

Inserting and Modifying Text

Correct Spelling and Grammar Usage
Use the Thesaurus

Word has a built-in thesaurus to help you when you need to find a synonym or an antonym for a word. You can access the thesaurus by right-clicking the word you want to replace or by using a command on the Tools menu.

If none of the Thesaurus suggestions is exactly the word you want, click Look Up in the dialog box to look up the synonym in the Replace with Synonym box to see more suggestions.

Activity Steps

open EWLetter08.doc

1. Select **asking** in the first line in the body of the letter

2. Click **Tools** on the menu bar, point to **Language**, then click **Thesaurus**

3. Click **Look Up** to look up the infinitive form of the verb, which appears in the Replace with Related Word box
See Figure 1-25.

4. Click **Replace** to replace the selected word in the document with the selected word in the Replace with Synonym box

5. Press **[Backspace]**, then type **ing**

6. Right-click **talk** in the last paragraph, point to **Synonyms** on the shortcut menu, then click **chat**, as shown in Figure 1-26

close EWLetter08.doc

Figure 1-25: **Thesaurus dialog box**

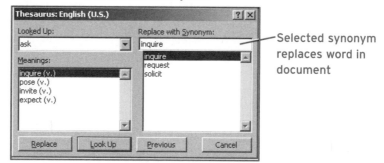

Selected synonym replaces word in document

Figure 1-26: **Looking up synonyms**

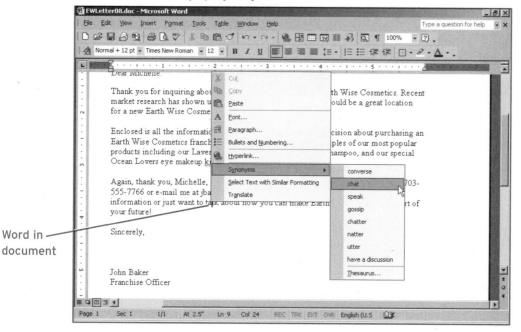

Word in document

Skill Set 1

Inserting and Modifying Text

Apply Font and Text Effects
Apply Character Effects

Formatting commands like Bold, Italic, and Underline are common and appear on the Formatting toolbar. You can apply additional formatting effects to your text if you use the Effects section in the Font dialog box. For example, you can add a line through text, shift text up or down for super- and subscripts, change text to all uppercase, and add interesting effects, such as a shadow, to text. In addition to the buttons on the Formatting toolbar, you can also open the Font dialog box and take advantage of a few additional formatting options.

Right-click selected text, then click Font on the shortcut menu to open the Font dialog box.

Activity Steps

 open EWCoDescription02.doc

1. Select **Earth Wise Cosmetics** in the first line

2. Click **Format** on the menu bar, then click **Font** to open the Font dialog box

3. Click the **Outline check box**, then click the **Small caps check box**
   See Figure 1-27.

4 Click **OK**

5. Select © in the fourth line in the paragraph under the heading **Company Background**

6. Open the Font dialog box, click the **Superscript check box**, click **OK**, then click in a blank area of the screen to deselect the text
   See Figure 1-28.

 close EWCoDescription02.doc

Figure 1-27: Font dialog box with text effects selected

Effects section of Font dialog box

Preview of formatted text

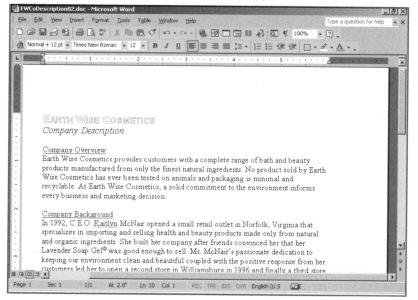

Figure 1-28: Document with text effects applied

Skill Set 1

Inserting and Modifying Text

Apply Font and Text Effects
Apply Text Animation

If you create a document that is going to be read primarily onscreen rather than in printed form, you can add text animations. Animations are special text effects that move onscreen. You add animation effects in the Font dialog box.

Do not use too many text animations in a document because they can distract the reader from your message.

Activity Steps

 open EWAnnouncement03.doc

1. Select the first line in the document

2. Right-click the selected text, click **Font** on the shortcut menu, then click the **Text Effects tab**

3. Click **Sparkle Text** in the Animations list, then watch the Preview box
   See Figure 1-29.

4. Click **OK**

5. Click anywhere in the document to deselect the text
   See Figure 1-30.

 close EWAnnouncement03.doc

Figure 1-29: Text Effects tab in the Font dialog box

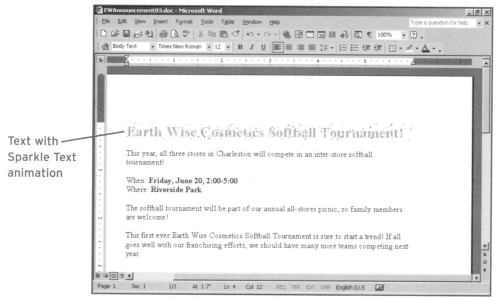

Figure 1-30: Text animation effect applied

Text with Sparkle Text animation

Skill Set 1

Inserting and Modifying Text

Apply Font and Text Effects
Apply Highlighting

Just as you would use a highlighting marker on paper documents, you can add highlighting to a Word document. Highlighting is easy to see when you are reading a document onscreen. If you want to print a document with highlighting, it's a good idea to use a light color for the highlight so that you can see the text underneath. To apply highlighting, you can select the text, then click the Highlight button list arrow and choose a highlight color, or you can click the Highlight button, and then drag it across the text you want to highlight.

Activity Steps

 open EWMemo02.doc

1. Select the phrase **wealth of valuable information** in the second paragraph in the body of the memo

2. Click the **Highlight button list arrow**

3. Click the **Yellow color box** to highlight the selected text

4. Click the **Highlight button** to activate it, then drag to highlight the phrase **you can use _____ to enhance your life** in the last line of the second paragraph
See Figure 1-31.

Step 6

You can also press [Esc] to turn the Highlighter off.

5. Click the **Highlight button list arrow** , click **None**, then drag to remove the highlighting from the words **you can use _____ to** in the last line of the second paragraph

6. Click the **Highlight button** to deselect it
See Figure 1-32.

close EWMemo02.doc

Figure 1-31: Highlighted text

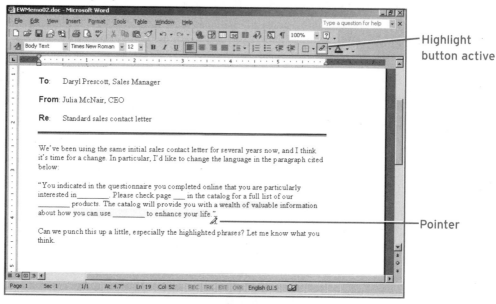

Highlight button active

Pointer

Figure 1-32: Highlight button deselected

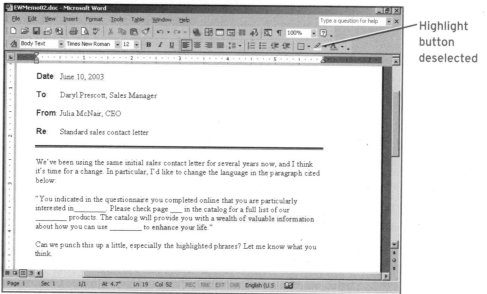

Highlight button deselected

Skill Set 1
Inserting and Modifying Text

Enter and Format Date and Time
Insert the Current Date and Time

Word makes it easy to insert the current date and time. You can insert them in two ways: either as static text that will not change, or as a date and time field that updates every time you open the document. A **field** is a placeholder for something that might change in a document. Fields are usually updated as the document changes.

To insert the current date using AutoText, type the first four characters of the current month, press [Enter], press the [Spacebar], then press [Enter] again.

Activity Steps

 open EWCoDescription03.doc

1. Click after **on:** in the third line (make sure there is a space between the colon and the insertion point)

2. Click **Insert** on the menu bar, click **Date and Time** to open the Date and Time dialog box, then click the third format in the list of Available formats
   See Figure 1-33.

3. If the **Update automatically check box** is selected, click it to deselect it so that the date in the document will not change, then click **OK**

4. Click after **Updated:** at the end of the third paragraph, immediately before the close parenthesis (make sure there is a space between the colon and the insertion point)

5. Click **Insert** on the menu bar, click **Date and Time**, then click the first format in the list of Available formats that shows the date and time (12th in the list)

6. Click the **Update automatically check box** to select it, then click **OK**
   See Figure 1-34.

 close EWCoDescription03.doc

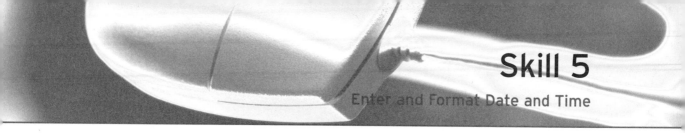

Figure 1-33: Date and Time dialog box

Select to update field
when file is opened

Figure 1-34: Date and time field in document

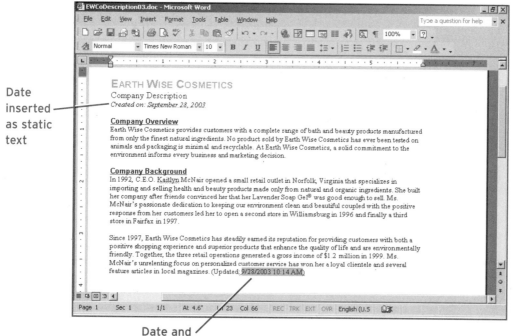

Date
inserted
as static
text

Date and
Time field

Skill Set 1

Inserting and Modifying Text

Enter and Format Date and Time
Modify Date and Time Field Formats

Once you've inserted a date or time, you can change it to a different format. For instance, if you inserted the date to be displayed in the format mm/dd/yy (for example, 06/04/03), you can change it to be displayed as text (for example, June 4, 2003).

Activity Steps

 open EWCoDescription04.doc

Once you've inserted the date and time, you can format it as you would any other text.

1. Position the insertion point so that it is immediately before the first number in the date at the end of the document

2. Press and hold **[Shift]**, then press **[➡]** to select the entire field
   See Figure 1-35.

3. Click **Insert** on the menu bar, then click **Date and Time**

4. Click the fourth format in the list of Available formats

5. If the **Update automatically check box** is not selected, click it to select it

6. Click **OK** to update the field with the new format

 close EWCoDescription04.doc

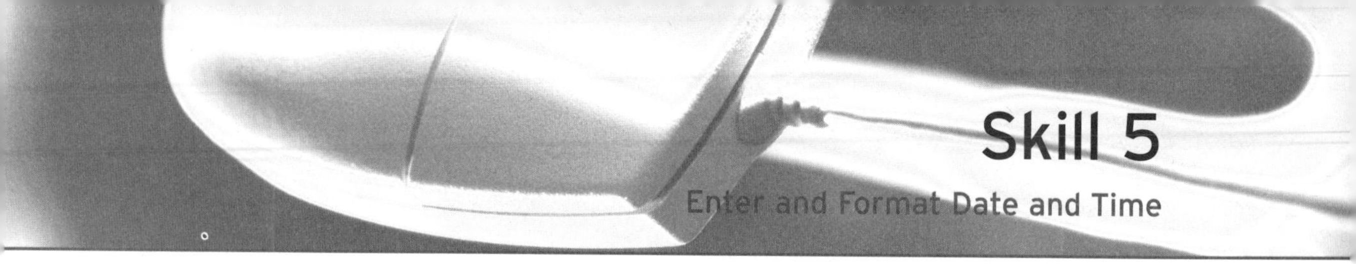

Figure 1-35: Selecting an entire field

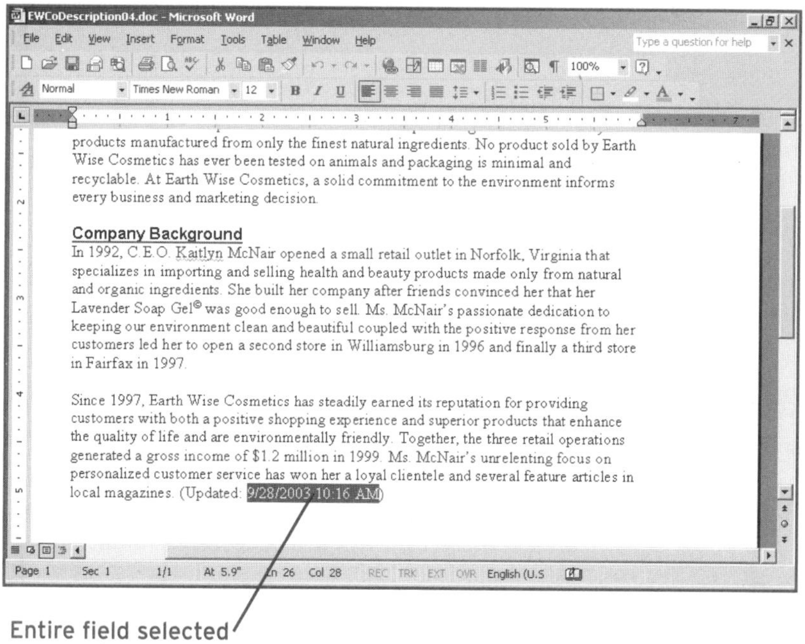

Entire field selected

extra!

Changing the date and time field codes

When the Date and Time is inserted into a document as a field instead of just simple text, you can modify the field codes to change how the date is displayed. Right-click the field, then click Toggle Field Codes to view the field codes instead of the result. Click anywhere in the code and make your changes. For example, if the date code contains the code M, the month number will display without a leading zero for single digit months (for example, 6 for June). You could change this to MM to display two digits for the month (06 for June), MMM to display a three letter abbreviation for the month (Jun), or MMMM to display the entire month name. Once you've made your changes, right-click the field again, then click Update Field to update the field and toggle back to the results.

Skill Set 1

Inserting and Modifying Text

Apply Character Styles

A **style** is a defined set of formats that is applied to text. If you want all the headings in your document to be 24 point, bold Arial, instead of selecting all of the text and then applying each of these formatting changes one at a time, you can apply a heading style that sets all three of these formats at once. Styles can be applied to characters and to paragraphs. When you apply a style, it overrides any formatting that was there previously. Word provides pre-defined styles from which you can choose.

Don't forget that to apply a character style, you must first select all the text to which you want to apply it.

Activity Steps

 open EWAnnouncement04.doc

1. Select the text **Earth Wise Cosmetics Softball Tournament** in the last paragraph

2. Click the **Style button list arrow** `Normal ▼`, then click **More** to open the Styles and Formatting task pane
   See Figure 1-36.

3. Click the **Show box list arrow** `Available formatting ▼` at the bottom of the Styles and Formatting task pane, then click **All styles** in the list

4. Scroll down the **Pick formatting to apply list** in the task pane, then click **Strong**

5. Select the text **first ever** in the last paragraph, scroll up the **Pick formatting to apply list**, then click **Emphasis**
   See Figure 1-37.

6. Click the **Styles and Formatting button** 🄰 to close the Styles and Formatting task pane

 close EWAnnouncement04.doc

Figure 1-36: Styles and Formatting task pane open

Click to open
and close Styles
and Formatting
task pane

Style button
arrow

Task pane

Format for
selected text

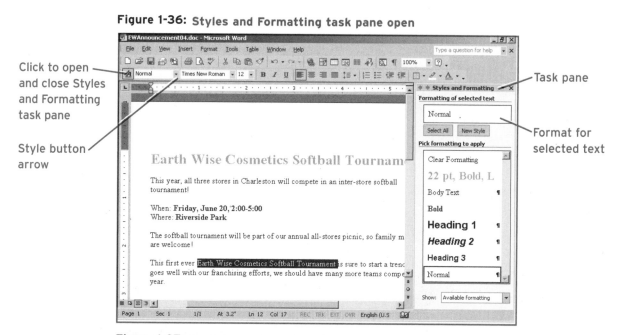

Figure 1-37: Applying a character style

"a" indicates
this is a
character style

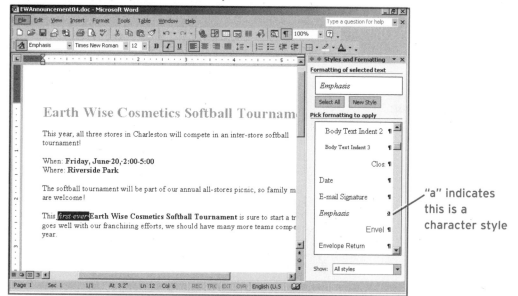

Skill Set 1

Inserting and Modifying Text

Target Your Skills

1 Use Figure 1-38 as a guide to create a new letter. Make sure you insert the current date as a field that will be updated each time the file is opened. Use the [Backspace] and [Delete] keys if you make any typing errors. Remember, don't worry if the lines don't wrap exactly as in the figure.

Figure 1-38

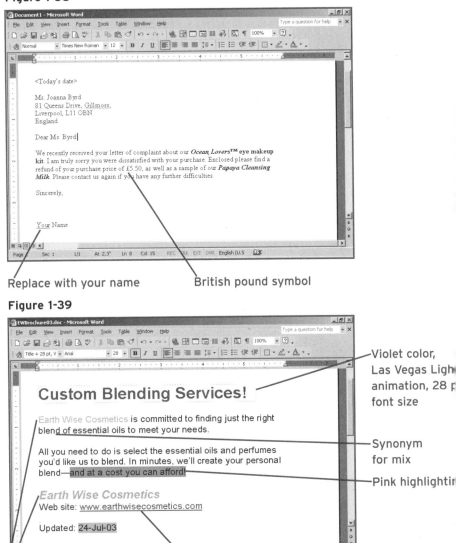

Replace with your name   British pound symbol

 **EWBrochure03.doc**

2 Use Figure 1-39 as a guide to create a final document. Use the spelling and grammar checker to get rid of any errors in the document. Note that the pargraph order is changed. Also note that you need to move, copy, or find a synonym for some of the words.

Figure 1-39

Violet color, Las Vegas Ligh animation, 28 p font size

Synonym for mix

Pink highlightir

Lavender color

Word formats Web addresses as blue and underlined automatically

Skill List

1. Modify paragraph formats
2. Set and modify tabs
3. Apply bullet, outline, and numbering format to paragraphs
4. Apply paragraph styles

In Skill Set 2, you learn how to work with paragraphs. Word provides many commands to format paragraphs. Most of the paragraph formatting commands are available on the toolbars, although a few can be accessed only from within dialog boxes. Using good paragraph formatting results in neat, professional-looking documents.

Once you've formatted a paragraph, the formatting remains even if you make modifications to the paragraph text. Using paragraph formatting allows you to avoid a lot of tedious adjusting with the [Spacebar] every time you change the text.

Skill Set 2
Creating and Modifying Paragraphs

Modify Paragraph Formats
Apply Paragraph Formats

To select a paragraph, place the insertion point anywhere within the paragraph. If you want to apply a format to more than one paragraph, you must select each paragraph. Once you have set a paragraph format, that format is applied to subsequent paragraphs when you press [Enter].

To insert blank space above and below individual paragraphs without pressing [Enter] twice, select the paragraphs, click Format on the menu bar, click Paragraph, then adjust the numbers in the Before and After boxes.

Activity Steps

 open EWMemo03.doc

1. Position the insertion point anywhere in the second paragraph in the body of the memo

2. Click the **Line Spacing (1) button list arrow**
   See Figure 2-1.

3. Click **2.0** in the Line Spacing button drop-down list to set the line spacing in the current paragraph to double-space

4. Position the insertion point after the period at the end of the second paragraph, then press **[Enter]** twice to start a new paragraph with the same formatting as the previous one

5. Type **The essential oils used in our new line of aromatherapy products will bring pleasure to your senses while nourishing and revitalizing your skin.**

6. Drag to select the second and third paragraphs, click the **Line Spacing button list arrow** , then click **1.5** in the drop-down list

7. Click anywhere in the document to deselect the text
   See Figure 2-2.

close EWMemo03.doc

extra!

Displaying paragraph symbols

The paragraph symbol, ¶, indicates the end of a paragraph. Sometimes it is easier to work with paragraph symbols displayed. To display paragraph symbols, click the Show/Hide ¶ button ¶. You can also click Options on the Tools menu, click the View tab, then select the Paragraph marks check box or the All check box in the Formatting marks section. Paragraph symbols are only viewable on screen; they are not printed.

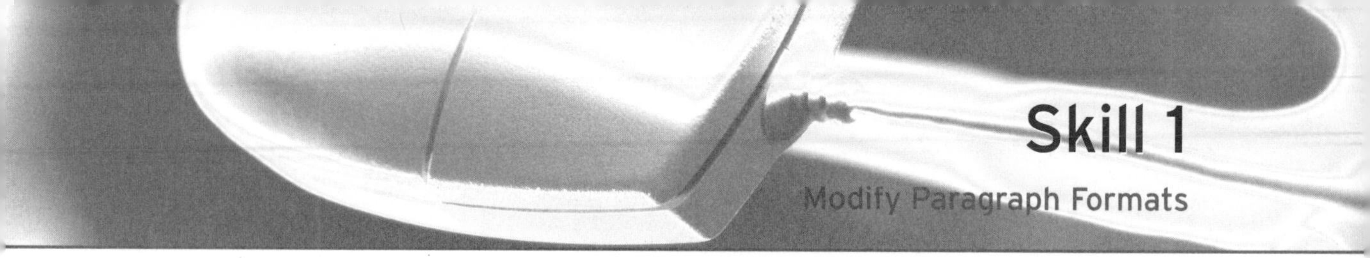

Figure 2-1: Setting paragraph line spacing

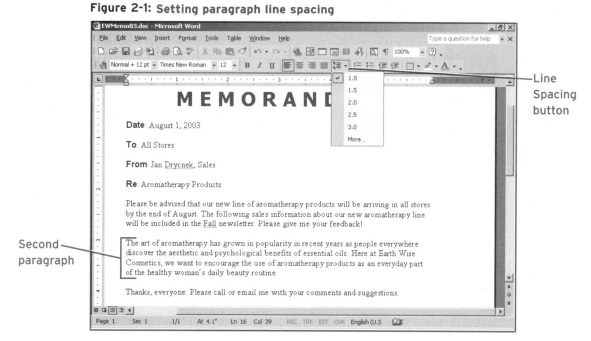

Second
paragraph

Line
Spacing
button

Figure 2-2: Paragraphs formatted differently

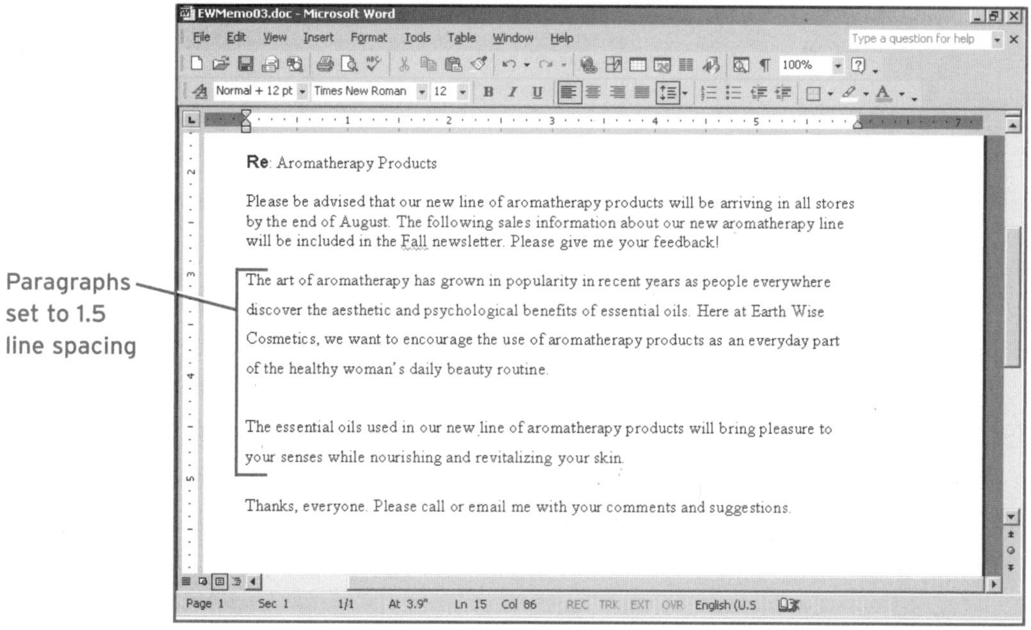

Paragraphs
set to 1.5
line spacing

Skill Set 2
Creating and Modifying Paragraphs

Modify Paragraph Formats
Modify Paragraph Alignment

Paragraphs can be **left-aligned** (aligned along the left margin), **right-aligned** (aligned along the right margin), **centered**, or **justified** (aligned along both the left and right margins). Left-aligned paragraphs are the easiest to read. Justified paragraphs are often used in books and newspapers because they look neater.

A paragraph that is left-aligned is sometimes called ragged right, because the right side of the paragraph is not aligned.

Activity Steps

open EWNewsletter01.doc

1. Make sure that the Insertion point is in the title line, **Earth Wise Cosmetics**, then note that the Align Left button is selected
2. Click the **Center button** to center the paragraph
3. Click anywhere in the second line on the page, **Fall 2003 Newsletter**, then click the **Align Right button**
4. Select the two paragraphs below the heading **Aromatherapy Products**, press and hold [Ctrl], then drag to select the paragraphs below **Franchise Opportunities** and below **Online Ordering**
5. Click the **Justify button** to justify all of the selected paragraphs
   See Figure 2-3.
6. Click anywhere in the document to deselect the text

close EWNewsletter01.doc

Figure 2-3: Paragraphs justified in document

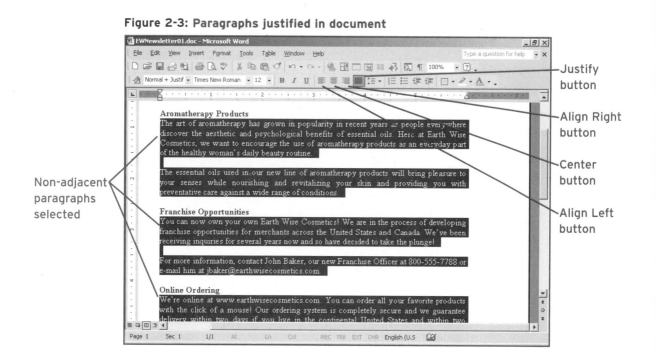

Justify button

Align Right button

Center button

Align Left button

Non-adjacent paragraphs selected

extra!

Using the Paragraph dialog box

To open the Paragraph dialog box click Paragraph on the Format menu (see Figure 2-4). The Paragraph dialog box contains the paragraph formatting commands available on the Formatting toolbar, as well as additional commands for formatting paragraphs. For example, to set the alignment from within the Paragraph dialog box, click the Alignment list arrow, then select an alignment option from the list.

Figure 2-4: Paragraph dialog box

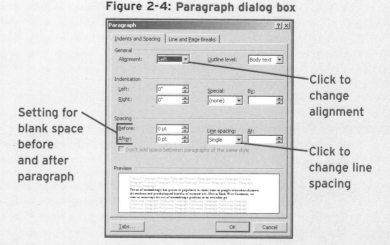

Click to change alignment

Setting for blank space before and after paragraph

Click to change line spacing

Skill Set 2
Creating and Modifying Paragraphs

Modify Paragraph Formats
Add Paragraph Borders and Shading

You may want to make a paragraph stand out from the rest of the paragraphs on the page. You can do this by adding a border or shading. You can also add borders to blank paragraphs to separate sections of a document visually.

Activity Steps

 open EWAnnouncement04.doc

1. With the insertion point positioned anywhere in the first line of text, click **Format** on the menu bar, click **Borders and Shading**, then click the **Borders tab**, if necessary

2. Click the **down scroll arrow** in the Style list six times, then click the line style that shows a thick line with a thin line above and below it

3. Click the **Color list arrow**, then click the **Dark Teal square** (first row, fifth box)

4. Click the **left, right,** and **top lines** in the Preview box so they disappear and the only remaining line is the bottom line
   See Figure 2-5.

5. Click **OK**

6. Scroll to the bottom of the page, select the paragraph that starts with **For more information**, click **Format** on the menu bar, click **Borders and Shading**, click the **Shading tab**, then click the **last gray square** in the top row below No Fill so that the indicator box to the right displays **Gray-30%**

7. Click **OK**, click anywhere in the document to deselect the text, click the **Zoom box list arrow** 100% ▾, then click **75%**
   See Figure 2-6.

 close EWAnnouncement04.doc

You can click the Outside Border button list arrow to apply a border.

Figure 2-5: Borders tab in the Borders and Shading dialog box

Selected line style

Dark teal selected

Sides and top do not have a border

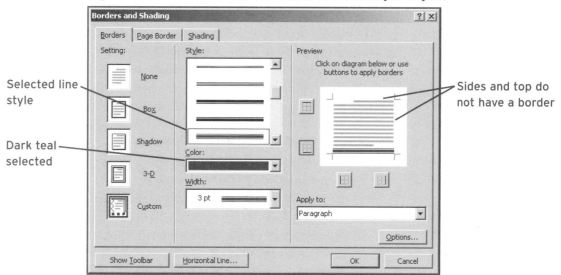

Figure 2-6: Paragraphs with a border and shading

Border added

Shading added

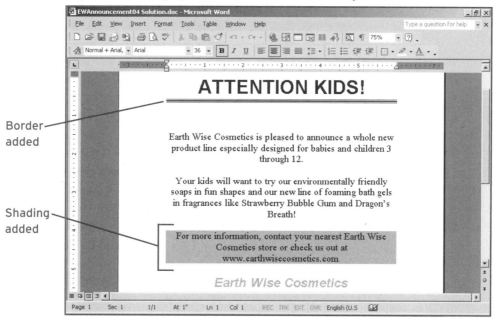

Skill Set 2

Creating and Modifying Paragraphs

Modify Paragraph Formats
Set First-line Indents

To visually indicate a new paragraph, you typically press [Enter] twice or set the line space after a paragraph so that there is a blank line between paragraphs. You can, of course, also indicate a new paragraph by indenting the first line. (Note: It's not good practice to both skip a line between paragraphs and indent the first line; do one or the other.)

Activity Steps

 open EWNewsletter02.doc

1. If the ruler is not displayed on your screen, click **View** on the menu bar, then click **Ruler**

2. Select the two paragraphs below the heading **Aromatherapy Products**

3. Click the **square** to the left of the ruler as many times as necessary to cycle through the selections until you see the **First Line Indent icon** ▽
   See Figure 2-7.

4. Click the **¹/₄" mark** on the ruler to place the First Line Indent marker at that point

5. Select the two paragraphs below the heading **Franchise Opportunities,** press and hold **[Ctrl]**, then select the two paragraphs below **Online Ordering**

6. Click the **¹/₄" mark** on the ruler to indent the first line of these selected paragraphs to ¹/₄" as well
   See Figure 2-8.

7. Click anywhere in the document to deselect the text

close EWNewsletter02.doc

Step 5
You may need to click the ¹/₄" mark on the ruler a second time to format all of the selected text.

Figure 2-7: Selecting a different ruler icon

First Line Indent icon

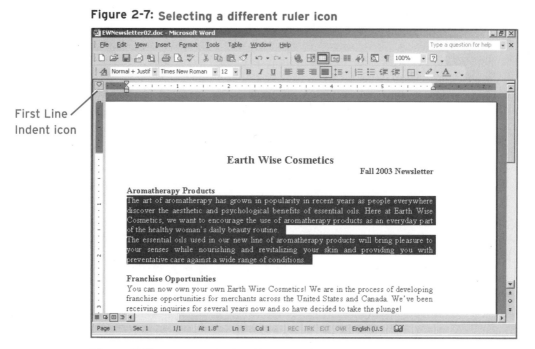

Figure 2-8: Document with first-line indents set

First Line Indent marker at ¹/₄" mark

First lines indented

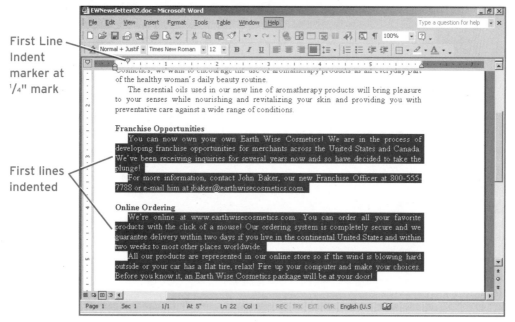

Skill Set 2
Creating and Modifying Paragraphs

Modify Paragraph Formats
Indent Entire Paragraphs

There may be times when you want to indent an entire paragraph in a document. You can click the Increase Indent button, or you can drag the Left and Right Indent Markers on the ruler.

Step 2
Click the Decrease Indent button to decrease the left indent by $1/2$".

Activity Steps

 open EWMemo04.doc

1. Select the three paragraphs in the body of the memo listing the promotion dates

2. Click the **Increase Indent button** 📋 to increase the indent by $1/2$" *See Figure 2-9.*

3. Position the pointer over the **Right Indent marker** △ on the right side of the ruler so that the ScreenTip appears

4. Drag the **Right Indent marker** △ to the left to the $5^1/2$" mark on the ruler as shown in Figure 2-10

5. Click anywhere in the document to deselect the text

 close EWMemo04.doc

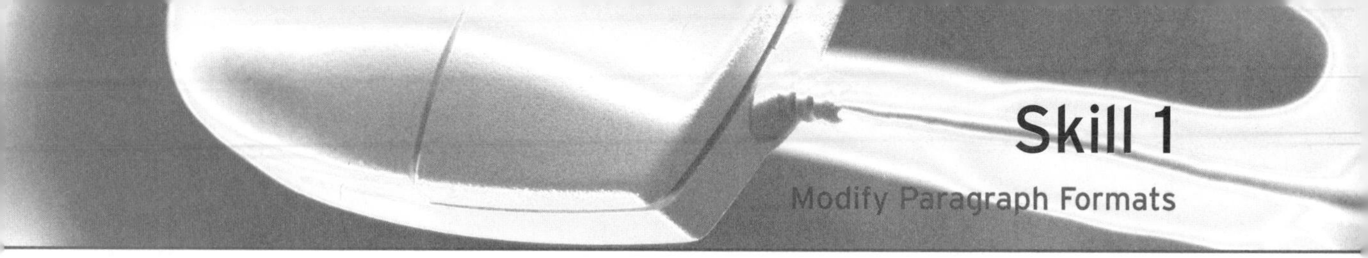

Figure 2-9: Paragraphs indented ½"

Selected paragraphs indented to ½" mark

Increase Indent button

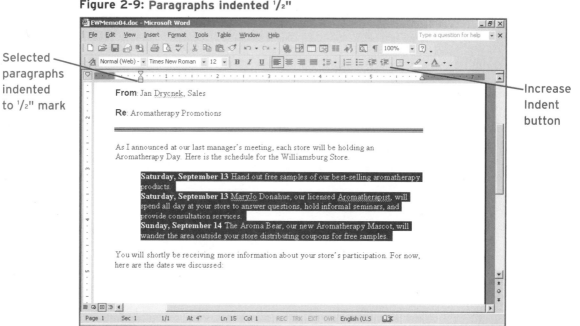

Figure 2-10: Dragging Right Indent marker to the 5½" mark

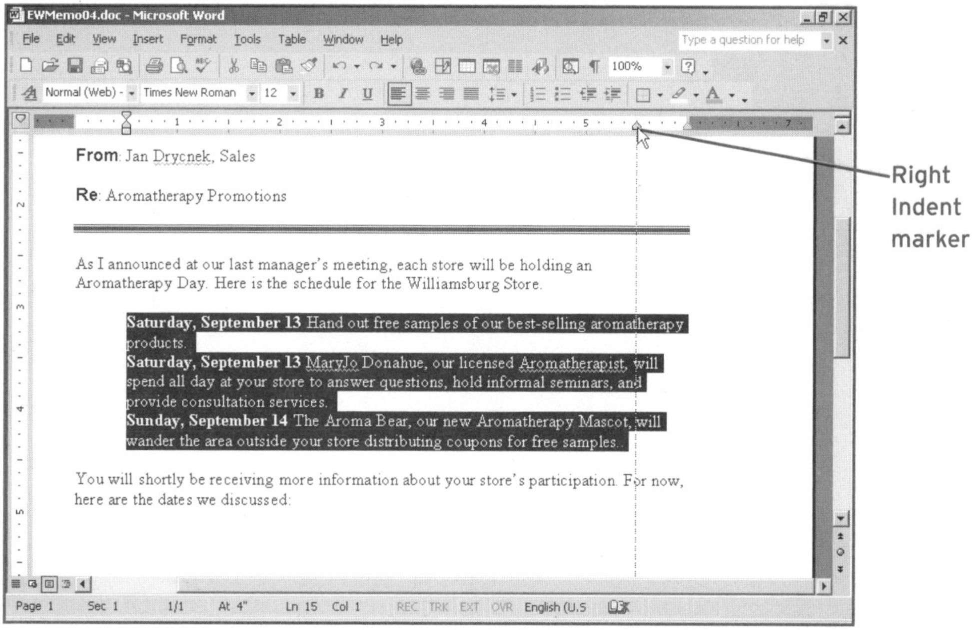

Right Indent marker

Skill Set 2
Creating and Modifying Paragraphs

Modify Paragraph Formats
Set Hanging Indents

A paragraph with a **hanging indent** is formatted so that all of the lines after the first line are indented more than the first line. You can set up a hanging indent by using the ruler or the Paragraph dialog box. Avoid trying to set up a hanging indent using the [Spacebar] and [Enter]. Any subsequent changes that you make to the document or to its format will alter the spacing you created by using the [Spacebar].

If you accidentally drag the Left Indent marker, either drag it back to the 0" mark on the ruler or click the Undo button.

Activity Steps

 open EWMemo05.doc

1. Select the three paragraphs in the body of the memo listing the promotion dates

2. Point to the Hanging Indent marker on left side of the ruler so that the ScreenTip appears
   See Figure 2-11.

3. Drag the Hanging Indent marker to the 2¹/₄" mark on the ruler
   See Figure 2-12.

4. Click anywhere in the document to deselect the text

close EWMemo05.doc

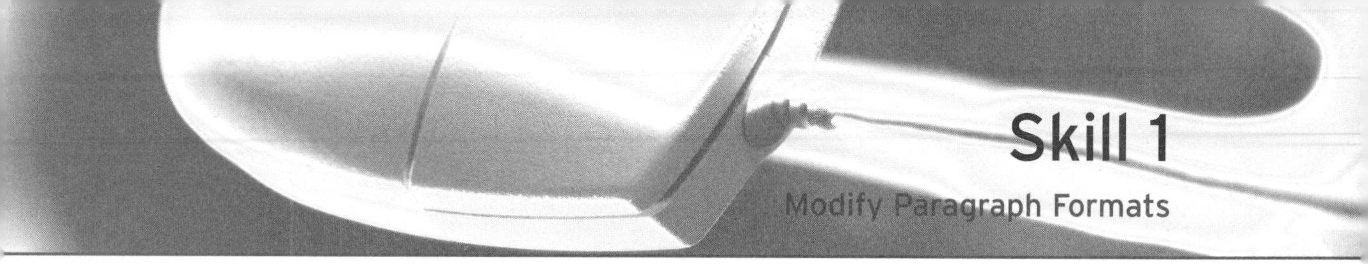

Figure 2-11: Finding the hanging indent marker

Hanging Indent marker

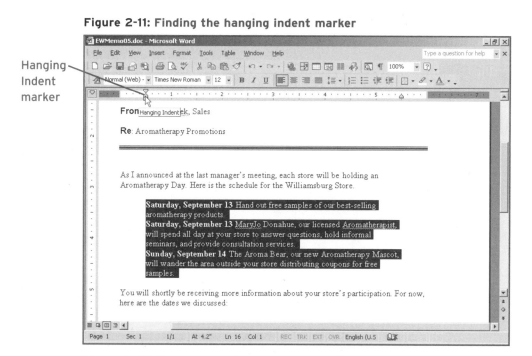

Figure 2-12: Paragraphs with hanging indents set

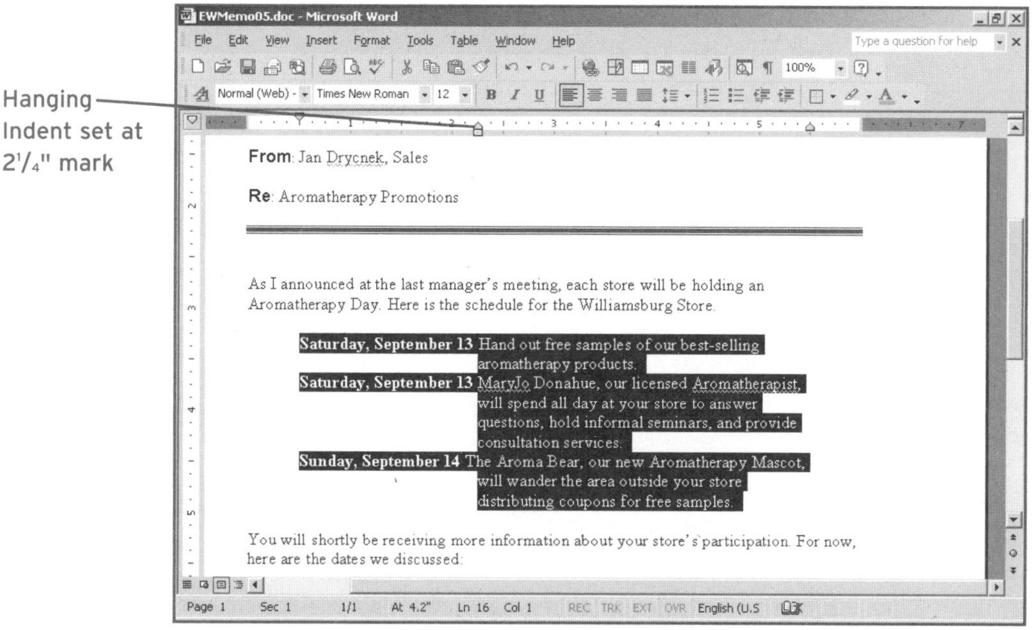

Hanging Indent set at 2¼" mark

Skill Set 2
Creating and Modifying Paragraphs

Set and Modify Tabs
Set Tabs

You use tabs to align text to the same point in different paragraphs. Default **tab stops**, the location on the ruler where the text moves when you press [Tab], are set every half-inch across the page.

If you accidentally click the ruler and place a new tab stop on it, just drag it off the ruler.

Activity Steps

 open EWMemo06.doc

1. Click immediately before **August** in the Date line, then press **[Backspace]** to delete the space after the colon

2. Press **[Tab]** to move the text over to the default tab stop at $1/2$"

3. Replace the spaces after the colons in the next three memo header lines with tabs
   See Figure 2-13.

4. Click the **square** to the left of the ruler as many times as necessary to cycle through the selections until you see the **Left Tab icon** [L]

5. Select the four memo header lines, starting with the Date line

6. Click the $3/4$" **mark** on the ruler to place a Left Tab stop and override the default tab setting in the selected paragraphs
   See Figure 2-14.

7. Click anywhere in the document to deselect the text

 close EWMemo06.doc

Figure 2-13: Tabs inserted in memo header paragraphs

Text aligned at default tab stop of ½"

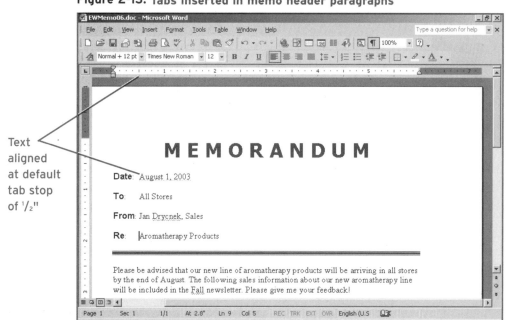

Figure 2-14: New tab stops set in memo header paragraphs

Inserted Left Tab stop overrides the default tab stop at ½"

Text aligned at new tab stop

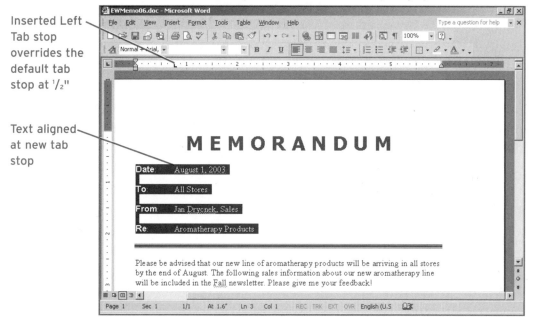

Skill Set 2

Creating and Modifying Paragraphs

Set and Modify Tabs
Modify Tabs

Once you have set tab stops, you can change them or delete them. You can also change the type of tab you set. For example, you can change from a left tab stop to a right tab stop.

Step 1
If tab markers don't appear when you click the Show/Hide ¶ button, click Options on the Tools menu, then click the Tab characters check box or the All check box to select it.

Activity Steps

 open EWAnnouncement05.doc

1. Click the **Show/Hide ¶ button** if necessary to display paragraph symbols and tab markers, then select the last four lines in the document

2. Drag the **Left Tab stop** ⌊ at the 3½" mark on the ruler off the ruler to delete it

3. Click the **square** to the left of the ruler as many times as necessary to cycle through the selections until you see the **Decimal Tab icon** ⌊

4. Click the 3³/₄" **mark** on the ruler to place a Decimal Tab stop

5. Drag the **Left Tab stop** ⌊ at the 4³/₄" mark off the ruler, then click the 5¼" **mark** on the ruler to place a Decimal Tab stop

6. Click anywhere in the first line of text, then click the **square** to the left of the ruler as many times as necessary to cycle through the selections until you see the **Right Tab icon** ⌋

7. Click just to the left of the **Right Indent marker** △ on the ruler to place the Right Tab stop, then drag the **Right Tab stop** ⌋ to the right so it is directly on top of the Right Indent marker
See Figure 2-15.

8. Click the **Show/Hide ¶ button** ¶ to turn off paragraph symbols and tab markers

close EWAnnouncement05.doc

Figure 2-15: Tabs modified

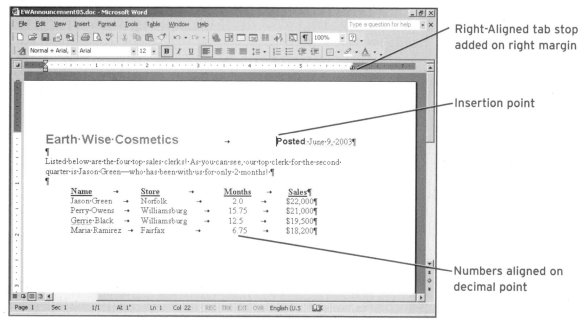

Right-Aligned tab stop added on right margin

Insertion point

Numbers aligned on decimal point

extra!

Using tab leaders

You can set a tab leader, a dotted, dashed, or solid line before a tab stop, by using the Tabs dialog box. Select the paragraphs in which you want to set the tab leaders, click Format on the menu bar, then click Tabs (see Figure 2-16). In the Tab stop position list, select the tab stop for which you want to set a leader, then click the leader style you want to use.

Figure 2-16: Tabs dialog box

Selected tab stop has a dotted line leader

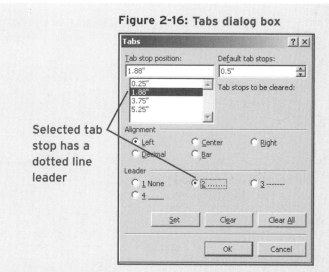

Skill Set 2
Creating and Modifying Paragraphs

Apply Bullet, Outline, and Numbering Format to Paragraphs
Create a Bulleted List

You can use bulleted lists for lists in which the order is not important, and no one item in the list is any more important than another. To create a bulleted list in Word, you can type the items in the list and then click the Bullets button, or you can click the Bullets button first, then start typing your list. A new bullet will be created every time you press [Enter] until you click the Bullets button again to turn the feature off.

Step 3
You can also click Bullets and Numbering on the Format menu to open the Bullets and Numbering dialog box.

Activity Steps

 open EWNewsletter03.doc

1. Select the five lines listing products, above the heading **Franchise Opportunities**

2. Click the **Bullets button** 📋

3. Right-click the selected list, then click **Bullets and Numbering** on the shortcut menu

4. Click **Customize**, then click **Character** to open the Symbol dialog box

5. Click the **Font list arrow**, scroll down the list, then click **Wingdings**

6. Scroll through the list, then click the bullet style shown in Figure 2-17

7. Click **OK**, click **OK** in the Customize Bulleted List dialog box, then click anywhere in the document to deselect the list
   See Figure 2-18.

 close EWNewsletter03.doc

---

extra!

Customizing bulleted lists
You can customize bulleted lists in several ways. You can change the bullet itself by choosing a different character, as you did in this skill, or, you can use a picture as a bullet by clicking Picture in the Bullets and Numbering dialog box. To make other changes, click Customize to open the Customize Bulleted List dialog box. There you can change the size of the bullet by clicking Font, and you can change the indent position of the bullet and the text by adjusting the measurements in the Indent at and Tab space after boxes.

Figure 2-17: Symbol dialog box

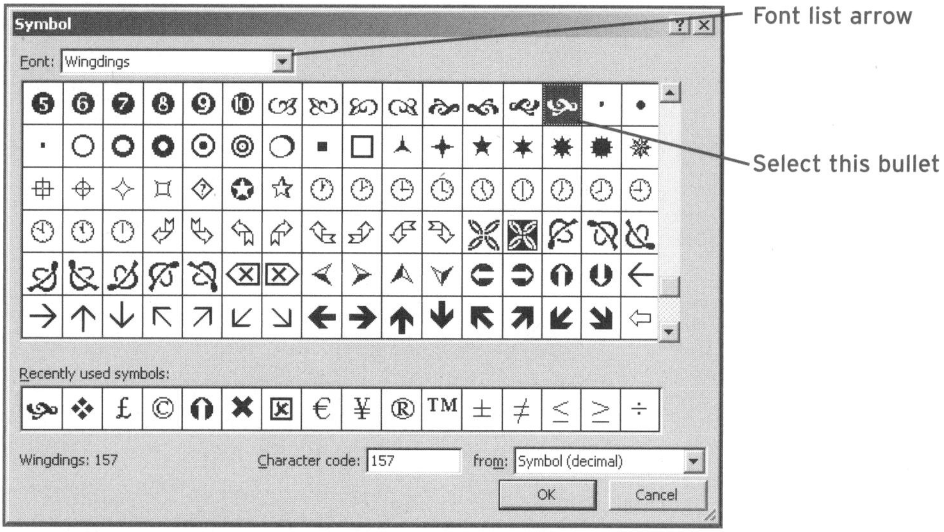

Font list arrow

Select this bullet

Figure 2-18: Bullets added to list

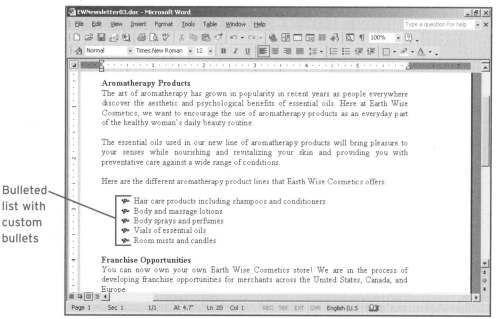

Bulleted list with custom bullets

Skill Set 2

Creating and Modifying Paragraphs

Apply Bullet, Outline, and Numbering Format to Paragraphs
Create a Numbered List

If you are working with a list in which the order is important or you need to be able to identify the items by a number, a numbered list is a better choice than a bulleted list.

Click the Number style list arrow in the Customize Numbered List dialog box to select another style of numbering, such as A, B, C or I, II, III.

Activity Steps

 open EWNewsletter04.doc

1. Scroll down to the bottom of the document, then select the last seven lines in the document
2. Click the **Numbering button** ▤
3. Right-click the **selected list**, then click **Bullets and Numbering** on the shortcut menu
4. Click **Customize**, click to the right of the entry in the **Number format box**, then press **[Backspace]** to delete the period after the number 1
   See Figure 2-19.
5. Click **Font**, click **Bold** in the Font style list, then click **OK** in the Font dialog box
6. Click **OK** in the Customize Numbered List dialog box, then click anywhere in the document to deselect the list
   See Figure 2-20.

 close EWNewsletter04.doc

Figure 2-19: Customize Numbered List dialog box

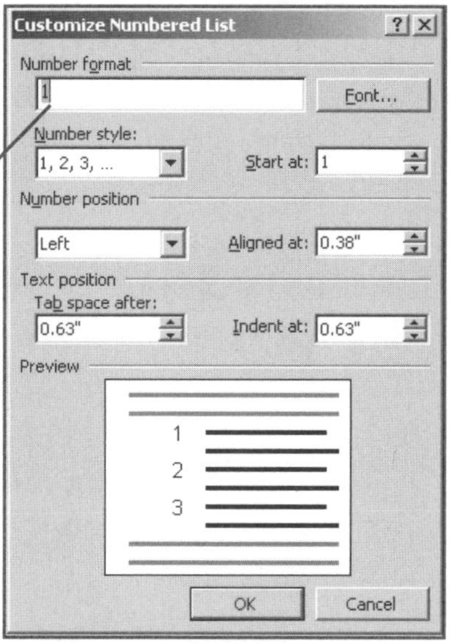

Period deleted

Figure 2-20: Numbers added to list

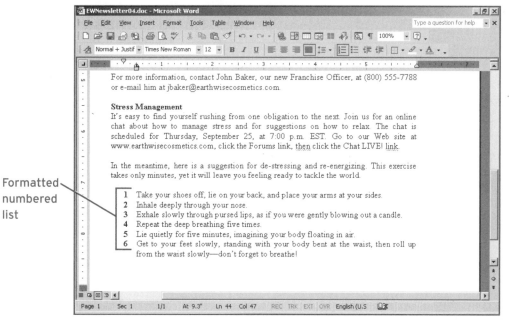

Formatted
numbered
list

Skill Set 2

Creating and Modifying Paragraphs

Apply Bullet, Outline, and Numbering Format to Paragraphs
Create a Numbered List in Outline Style

A numbered list can be set up in standard outline style: a list of topics and sub-topics with each topic numbered according to its position in the outline and its level. You can create an automatically numbered outline using the Numbering command.

You can press [Tab] to increase the indent of an existing outline item and indent it to the next level, or you can press [Shift][Tab] to decrease the indent level of an existing outline item.

Activity Steps

 open EWProposal01.doc

1. Select all of the text except the two title lines

2. Click **Format** on the menu bar, click **Bullets and Numbering**, then click the **Outline Numbered tab**

3. Click the second style in the first row
   See Figure 2-21.

4. Click **OK**

5. Click anywhere in the **Benefits** line in the middle of the list, then click the **Increase Indent button** to move it down a level

6. Click anywhere in the **Financial Considerations** line in the last line, then click the **Decrease Indent button** to move it up a level

7. Click after the word **Considerations** in the last line, press **[Enter]**, press **[Tab]**, type **Projected Revenues**, press **[Enter]**, then type **Liabilities**

8. Press **[Enter]**, press **[Shift][Tab]**, then type **Conclusion**
   See Figure 2-22.

 close EWProposal01.doc

Skill 3

Apply Bullet, Outline, and Numbering Format to Paragraphs

Figure 2-21: Outline Numbered tab in the Bullets and Numbering dialog box

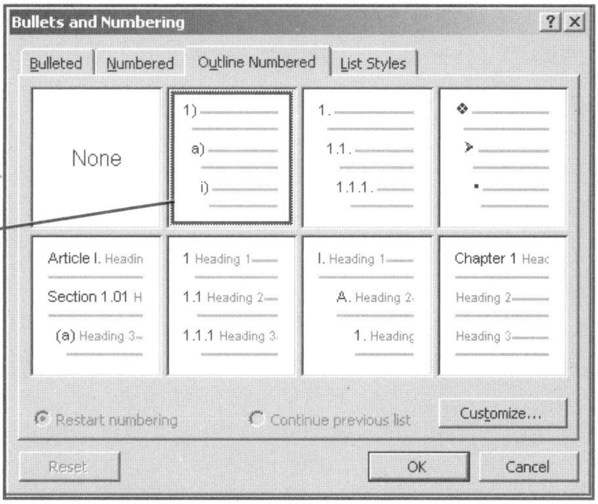

Select this style (it may be in a different spot on your screen)

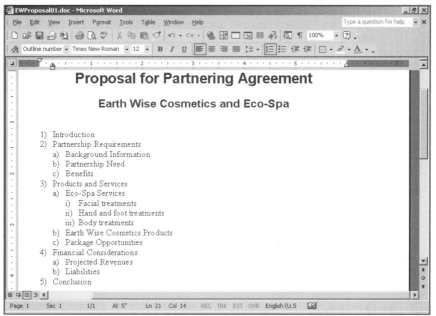

Figure 2-22: Numbered outline

Skill Set 2

Creating and Modifying Paragraphs

Apply Paragraph Styles

To make it easier to apply consistent formatting throughout a document, you can use paragraph styles. Remember, a style is a defined set of formats. Just as character styles are applied to selected text, paragraph styles are applied to entire paragraphs.

Step 7
When you modify a style with manual formatting, the formats you add are listed after the style name in the Style list box.

Activity Steps

 open EWNewsletter05.doc

1. Click anywhere in the **Aromatherapy Products** line, then click the **Style list arrow** `Normal ▾`

2. Click **Heading 1** in the Style list as shown in Figure 2-23 to apply the Heading 1 style to the paragraph

3. Apply the Heading 1 style to the lines **Franchise Opportunities** and **Stress Management**

4. Click anywhere in the first line of the document, then click the **Styles and Formatting button** `⧉` to open the Styles and Formatting task pane

5. Click the **Show list arrow** `Available formatting ▾` at the bottom of the task pane, click **All Styles**, scroll to the bottom of the **Pick formatting to apply list** in the task pane, then click **Title**

6. Click anywhere in the **Fall 2003 Newsletter** line, then apply the **Heading 3 style** using either the task pane or the toolbar

7. With the Fall 2003 Newsletter line still selected, click the **Align Right button** `≣`
   See Figure 2-24.

8. Click the **Close button** `✕` in the Styles and Formatting task pane title bar

 close EWNewsletter05.doc

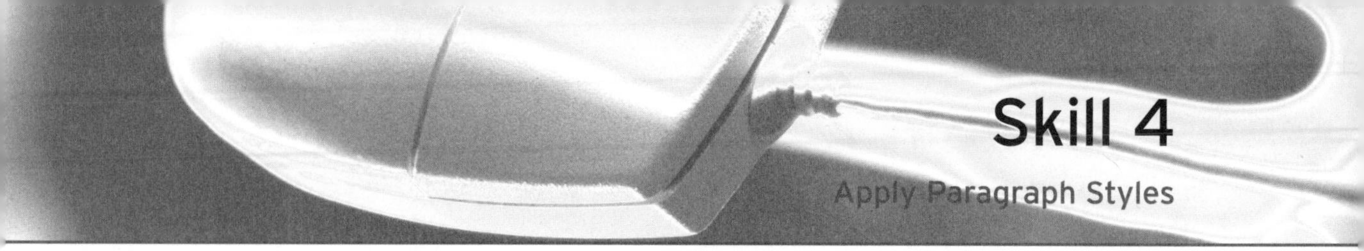

Figure 2-23: Style list on the Formatting toolbar

Style list arrow

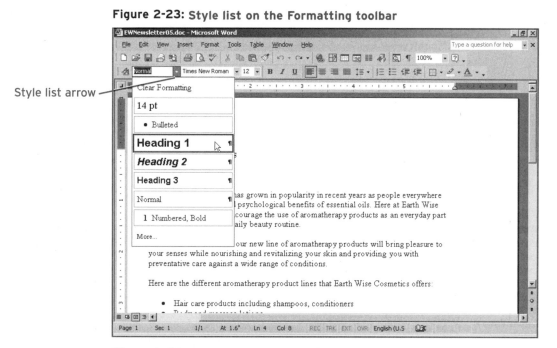

Figure 2-24: Document with styles applied

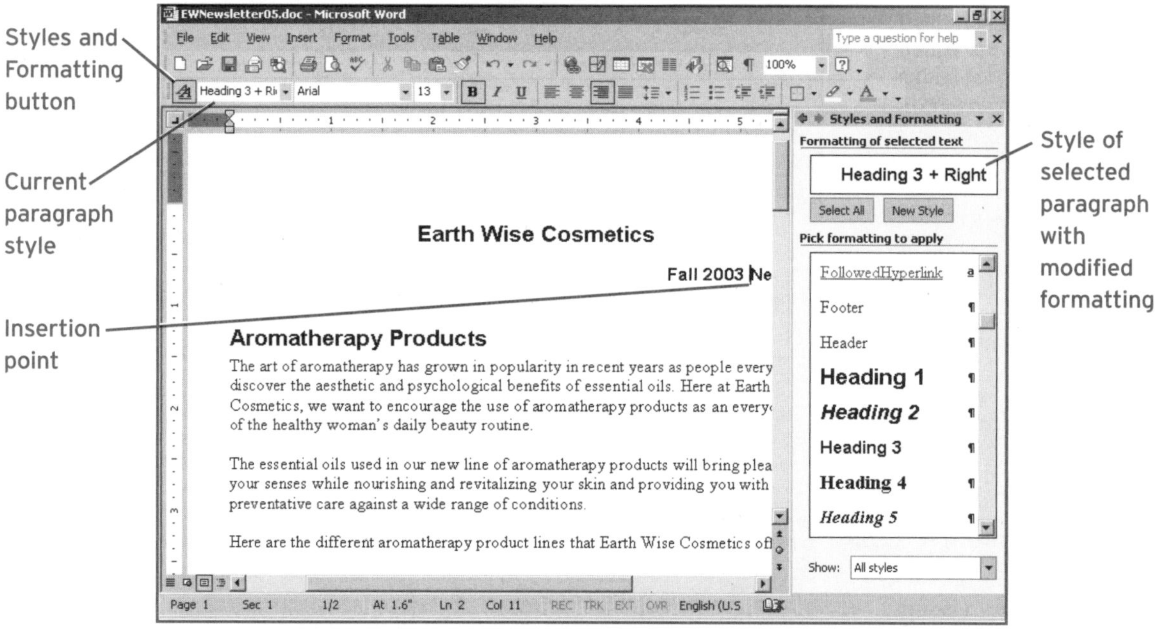

Styles and Formatting button

Current paragraph style

Insertion point

Style of selected paragraph with modified formatting

Skill Set 2

Creating and Modifying Paragraphs

Target Your Skills

 EWAnnouncement06.doc

1 Modify the file **EWAnnouncement06** to create the document shown in Figure 2-25. Paragraph marks are turned on to help you format the document correctly.

Figure 2-25

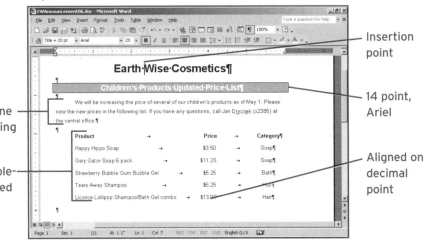

1.5 line spacing

Double-spaced

Insertion point

14 point, Ariel

Aligned on decimal point

 EWBrochure04.doc

2 Revise the **EWBrochure04** file to create the document shown in Figure 2-26. Paragraph marks are turned on to help you format the document correctly.

Figure 2-26

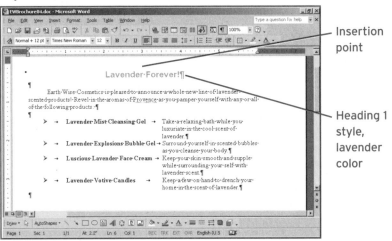

Insertion point

Heading 1 style, lavender color

Skill List

1. Create and modify a header and footer
2. Apply and modify column settings
3. Modify document layout and page setup options
4. Create and modify tables
5. Preview and print documents, envelopes, and labels

Once you've formatted the words and paragraphs in a document, you can think about the document as a whole. Adding headers and footers to a document can help the reader keep printed documents organized. You will learn how to add the filename, date, page numbers, and custom text to the header or footer. Sometimes a document is best laid out in more than one column, as in a newsletter. You will also learn how to set up a document with more than one column.

If you have quite a bit of information that would look better in multiple rows and columns, a table might be the best way to present it. You will learn how to insert a table into your document and modify it to fit your needs. Finally, you will learn to preview and print your document, as well as envelopes and labels.

Skill Set 3
Formatting Documents

Create and Modify a Header and Footer
Create a Header

A **header** is text that appears at the top of every page in a document. Headers can be very useful in a multiple-page document. You can insert **fields**, placeholders that will update automatically to match specific information like a page number or a date, or you can insert text that you type directly. Text in a header can be formatted just as any other text in a document.

You must be in Print Layout view or Print Preview to see headers and footers on the page.

Activity Steps

 open GCMemo01.doc

1. Click **View** on the menu bar, then click **Header and Footer**

2. Type **Draft Copy**, then click the **Align Right button** ▤

3. Press **[Enter]**

4. Click the **Insert Date button** 🗓 on the Header and Footer toolbar
   See Figure 3-1.

5. Select the two lines of text you entered, click the **Bold button** **B**, then click anywhere in the header area to deselect the text

6. Click the **Close button** on the Header and Footer toolbar
   See Figure 3-2.

 close GCMemo01.doc

Figure 3-1: Creating a header and using the Header and Footer toolbar

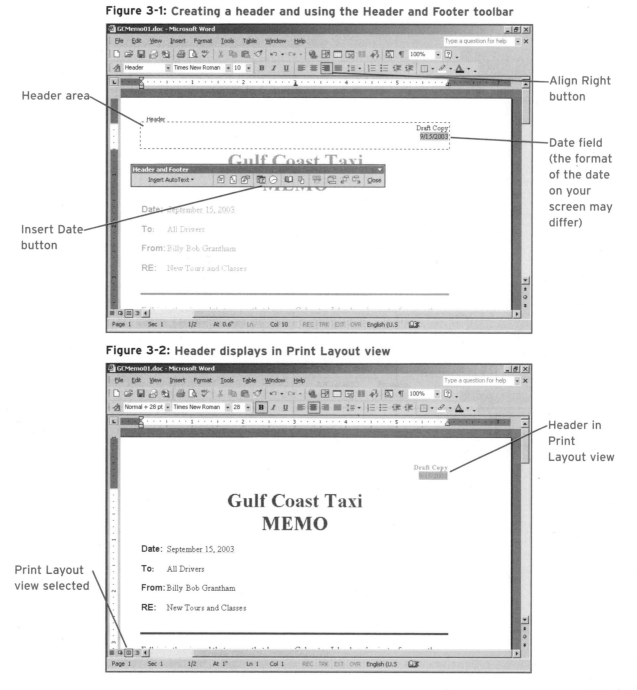

Header area

Insert Date
button

Align Right
button

Date field
(the format
of the date
on your
screen may
differ)

Figure 3-2: Header displays in Print Layout view

Header in
Print
Layout view

Print Layout
view selected

Skill Set 3
Formatting Documents

Create and Modify a Header and Footer
Create a Footer

A **footer** is text that appears at the bottom of every page in a document. Footers are identical to headers, except that they appear at the bottom of a page instead of the top.

Activity Steps

To insert the current page number and the total number of pages quickly, click the Insert AutoText button on the Header and Footer toolbar, then click Page X of Y.

file▶ open GCMemo02.doc

1. Click **View** on the menu bar, then click **Header and Footer**

2. Click the **Switch Between Header and Footer button** ⊞ on the Header and Footer toolbar to jump to the Footer area

3. Click the **Insert AutoText button** on the Header and Footer toolbar

4. Click **Filename** to insert the filename in the footer

5. Press **[Tab]** twice, then type **Gulf Coast Taxi Company Memo**
   See Figure 3-3.

6. Click the **Close button** on the Header and Footer toolbar, then scroll down to see the footer on the page
   See Figure 3-4.

file▶ close GCMemo02.doc

Figure 3-3: Inserting the Filename field in a footer

Insert Auto text button

Filename field in footer

Switch Between Header and Footer button

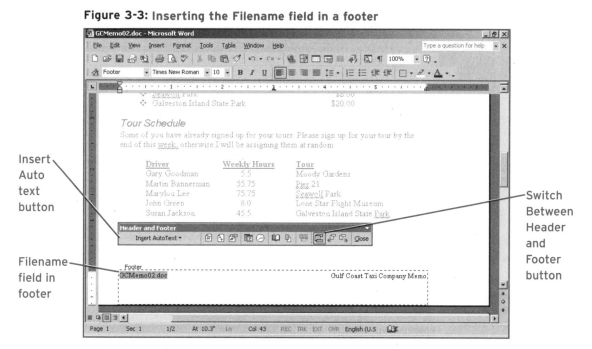

Figure 3-4: Viewing headers and footers on two pages in Print Layout view

Footer in Print Layout view

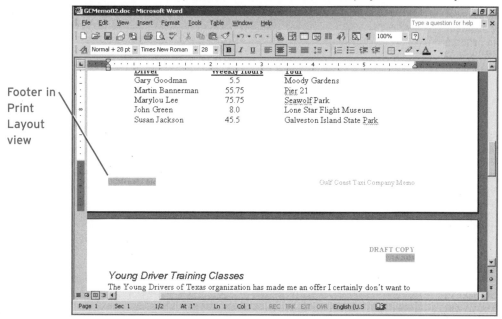

Skill Set 3
Formatting Documents

Apply and Modify Column Settings
Create Columns for Existing Text

Text in a document normally appears in one column. You may decide that the text would be easier to read or that you could fit more text if you used two or more columns. Newsletters are frequently set up in this way. The easiest way to create columns is to enter your text, then use the Columns command. You can choose to apply as many columns as you want.

Activity Steps

file ► open GCBrochure01.doc

1. Select all of the text below the line **Spring 2003**

2. Click the **Columns button**

3. Point to the **second column icon** in the drop-down list so that **2 Columns** appears below the icons
   See Figure 3-5.

4. Click the **second column icon** in the Columns button drop-down list

5. Click anywhere in the document to deselect the text

6. Click the **Zoom button list arrow** `100%` ▾ then click **Whole Page** to see the columns on the page
   See Figure 3-6.

file ► close GCBrochure01.doc

tip

If you want to format the entire document with multiple columns, click Select All on the Edit menu before you click the Columns button.

extra!

Understanding sections
When you apply the Columns command to selected text, you created a second section in the GCBrochure01 document. **Sections** are parts of a document with separate page formatting options. If you turn on paragraph marks, you can see a double-dotted line labeled **Section Break (Continuous)** next to the heading line **Spring 2003**. Everything after that break—everything in the second section of the document—has a different page format from the text in the first section in the document. You can have as many sections as you want in a document.

Figure 3-5: Using the Columns button

Columns button

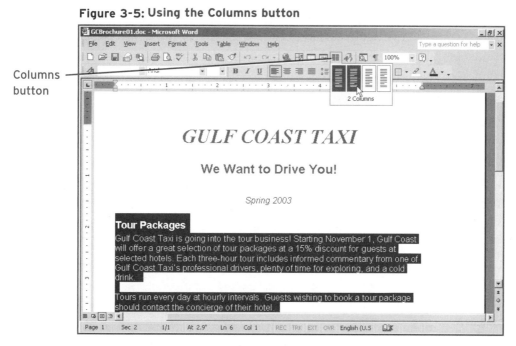

Figure 3-6: Document formatted with two columns

Formatted as single column

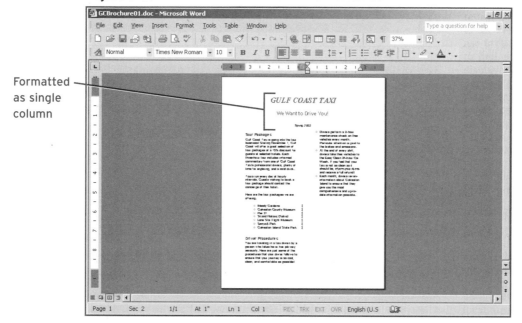

Skill Set 3

Formatting Documents

Apply and Modify Column Settings
Modify Text Alignment in Columns

Once you have created columns, you need to adjust them so that they look balanced on the page; in other words, so that you don't have one column that fills the length of the page and a second column that contains only a few lines.

To insert a vertical line between columns, make sure the insertion point is anywhere within the columns, click Columns on the Format menu, then click the Line between check box to select it.

Activity Steps

open GCBrochure02.doc

1. Click the **Zoom button list arrow** 100% ▾ on the menu bar, then click **Whole Page** to see the columns

2. Click below the text in the second column (the insertion point will seem to appear between the columns)

3. Click **Insert** on the menu bar, then click **Break** to open the Break dialog box

4. Click the **Continuous option button**

5. Click **OK** to balance the columns on the page
See Figure 3-7.

close GCBrochure02.doc

Using the Columns dialog box
In addition to using the Columns button, you can click Columns on the Format menu to open and use the Columns dialog box to set and modify columns. See Figure 3-8. If you want to format the document with one column in one section and two columns in another, position the insertion point in the document at the point where you want to start the new column layout, open the Columns dialog box, select the number of columns you want, then click the Apply to list arrow at the bottom of the dialog box and select This point forward. You can also precisely adjust the column width and space between each column by typing measurements (in inches) in the Width and Spacing boxes. Deselect the Equal column width check box if you want columns of different widths.

extra!

Skill 2

Apply and Modify Column Settings

Figure 3-7: Balanced newsletter columns

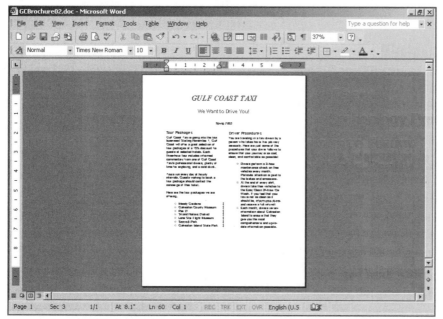

Figure 3-8: Columns dialog box

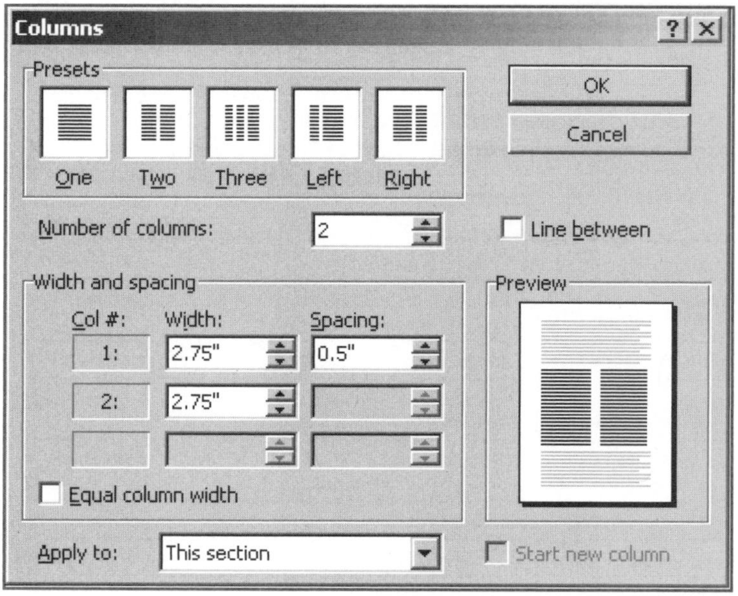

Skill Set 3
Formatting Documents

Apply and Modify Column Settings
Create Columns before Entering Text

If you know before you enter text that you want it to appear in two or more columns, you can use the Columns command before you enter the text. Note that if you start with a blank document, choosing the Columns command applies to all of the text in the document, even if you type a few lines first for a headline. So after you finish typing the text for your columns, you need to select the headline and format it with one-column layout.

To force a new column to start, position the insertion point at the point in the document where you want to start the new column, click Break on the Insert menu, then click the Column break option button.

Activity Steps

1. Open a new, blank document, change the zoom to 100% if necessary, click the **Style list arrow** |Normal ▼|, click **Heading 1**, type **Gulf Coast Taxi Newsletter**, then press **[Enter]**

2. Click the **Style list arrow** |Normal ▼|, click **Heading 3**, type **Summer 2003**, then press **[Enter]**

3. Click the **Columns button** ▦, then click the **second column icon** to format the text in two columns

4. Click the **Style list arrow** |Normal ▼|, click **Heading 1**, type **Employee News**, then press **[Enter]**

5. Type **Elisa Newcomb was married last weekend to Frank Jessup. Believe it or not, the happy couple met in Elisa's cab!** *See Figure 3-9.*

6. Select the first two paragraphs (everything above **Employee News**), click the **Columns button** ▦, then click the **first column icon** to format the selected text in one column

7. Click the **Center button** ▤ to center the title over the two columns

8. Click anywhere in the document to deselect the text *See Figure 3-10.*

 close file

Figure 3-9: Text filling in first column in two-column format

Second column not yet filled

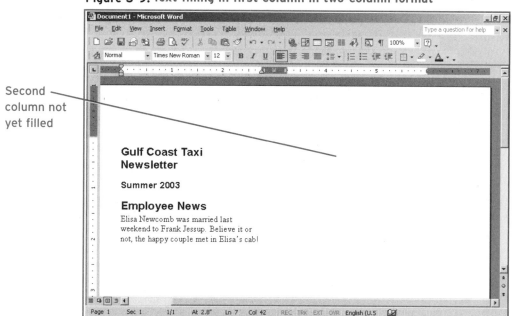

Figure 3-10: Headline spanning two columns

Paragraphs formatted as single column

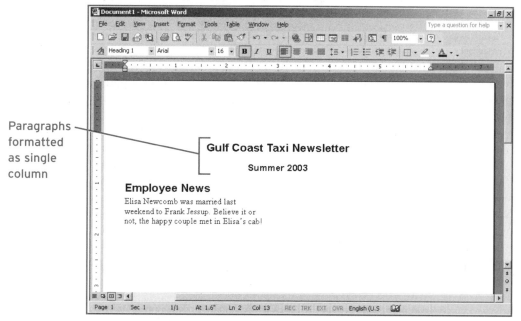

Skill Set 3
Formatting Documents

Apply and Modify Column Settings
Revise Column Layout

The default space between columns in a Word document is ¹/₂". The column widths change depending on how many columns are on a page. You can adjust both the column width and the space between columns. If you want to see the columns as you change the width, drag the Move Column markers on the ruler. To adjust columns precisely, you should use the Columns dialog box.

To create two columns quickly with one of the columns twice as wide as the other, select the text, click Columns on the Format menu, then click Left or Right at the top of the dialog box.

Activity Steps

 open GCBrochure03.doc

1. Scroll down until you can see the bulleted list of tour packages in the first column, then click anywhere in the first column

2. Position the pointer over the **Move Column dotted box marker** between the 2" and 3" markers on the ruler so that the pointer changes to ↔

3. Drag the **Move Column dotted box marker** to the right until it's approximately over the 3.25" mark on the ruler and the list of tours and the fees charged in the first column appears with each fee on the same line as the tour name
See Figure 3-11.

4. Click **Format** on the menu bar, then click **Columns** to open the Columns dialog box

5. Drag to select all of the text in the **Col # 2 Width box**, then type **1.6**

6. Press **[Tab]**, type **.3** to decrease the space between the second and third columns, then press **[Tab]** to adjust the width in the Col # 3 Width box automatically

7. Click **OK** to close the Columns dialog box

8. Click the **Zoom button list arrow** 100% ▾ , then click **Whole Page**
See Figure 3-12.

 close GCBrochure03.doc

Figure 3-11: Widening a column using the ruler

Drag to change column width

Drag to change space between columns

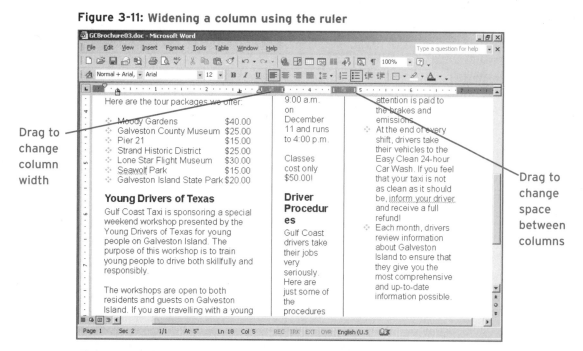

Figure 3-12: Newsletter with column widths adjusted

First column widened

Space between second and third columns narrowed

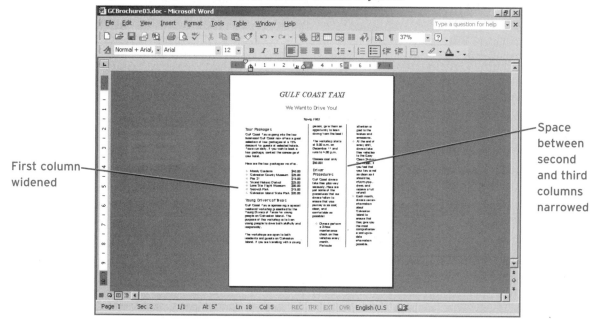

Skill Set 3
Formatting Documents

Modify Document Layout and Page Setup Options

Insert Page Breaks

Word automatically inserts page breaks in a document when the text will no longer fit on one page. You can insert page breaks manually if you want to start the next page at a different point in the document. In Print Layout view, manual page breaks look the same as automatic page breaks unless you turn on paragraph marks.

To delete a manually inserted page break, turn on paragraph marks, select the dotted line page break indicator, then press [Delete].

Activity Steps

 open GCProposal01.doc

1. Click the **Show/Hide ¶ button** ¶ to display paragraph marks, if necessary

2. Scroll down so that you can see the heading **Introduction**

3. Click at the beginning of the **Introduction** line to position the insertion point at the top of the new page you want to create

4. Click **Insert** on the menu bar, then click **Break** to open the Break dialog box

5. Make sure that the **Page break option button** is selected, then click **OK** to insert a manual page break
   See Figure 3-13.

6. Scroll down until you see the heading **Conclusion**

7. Click at the beginning of the **Conclusion** line, then press **[Ctrl][Enter]** to insert a manual page break

 close GCProposal01.doc

Figure 3-13: Manual page break

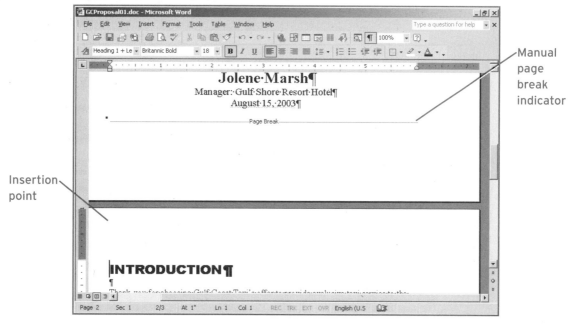

Manual page break indicator

Insertion point

extra!

Inserting section breaks

To create manual section breaks, click Break on the Insert menu, then select one of the option buttons under Section break types in the Break dialog box. See Figure 3-14. Clicking the Next page option button forces the new section to start on a new page. Clicking the Continuous option button creates a new section but keeps it on the same page. Clicking the Even and Odd page option buttons creates a new section that begins on the next even or odd-numbered page.

Figure 3-14: Break dialog box

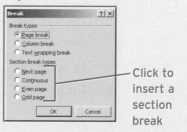

Click to insert a section break

Skill Set 3

Formatting Documents

Modify Document Layout and Page Setup Options
Insert Page Numbers

When you work with multiple-page documents, it's a good idea to add page numbers so that you don't mix up the pages when you print the document. To insert page numbers, you insert a field, and Word automatically updates the field to reflect the correct page number. You can insert page numbers using the Insert Page Number button on the Header and Footer toolbar or you can use the Page Numbers command on the Insert menu.

To format the page number, make the footer area active, then select the page number field and format it as you like.

Activity Steps

 open GCProposal02.doc

1. Click Insert on the menu bar, then click Page Numbers to open the Page Numbers dialog box

2. Make sure that Bottom of page (Footer) is selected in the Position list box

3. Click the Alignment list arrow, then click Left

4. Click the Show number on first page check box to deselect it
   See Figure 3-15.

5. Click OK

6. Scroll down to the bottom of the first page to see that there is no page number in the footer

7. Scroll down to the bottom of the second page to see the page number in the footer
   See Figure 3-16.

 close GCProposal02.doc

Figure 3-15: Page Numbers dialog box

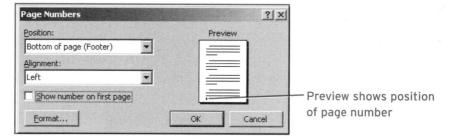

Preview shows position
of page number

Figure 3-16: Page number in footer of page 2

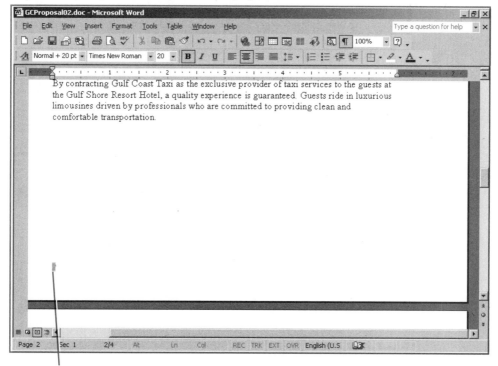

By contracting Gulf Coast Taxi as the exclusive provider of taxi services to the guests at the Gulf Shore Resort Hotel, a quality experience is guaranteed. Guests ride in luxurious limousines driven by professionals who are committed to providing clean and comfortable transportation.

Page number in
footer of page 2

Skill Set 3
Formatting Documents

Modify Document Layout and Page Setup Options
Modify Page Margins

The default page margins in a Word document are 1" at the top and bottom of the page and 1¼" at the right and left of the page. Headers and footers print ½" from the top and bottom of the page. You can change the default page margins to suit your needs.

To adjust text to fit on a page quickly, click the Print Preview button, then click the Shrink to Fit button on the Print Preview toolbar.

Activity Steps

 open GCLetter01.doc

1. Click **File** on the menu bar, then click **Page Setup**
2. Click the **Margins tab**, if necessary
3. Type **1.25** in the Top box
4. Press **[Tab]** twice to select the text in the Left box, then type **1.5**
5. Click the **Right box down arrow** three times to change the right margin to 1"
   See Figure 3-17.
6. Click **OK**
   See Figure 3-18.

 close GCLetter01.doc

Figure 3-17: Margins tab of the Page Setup dialog box

Figure 3-18: Margins changed in document

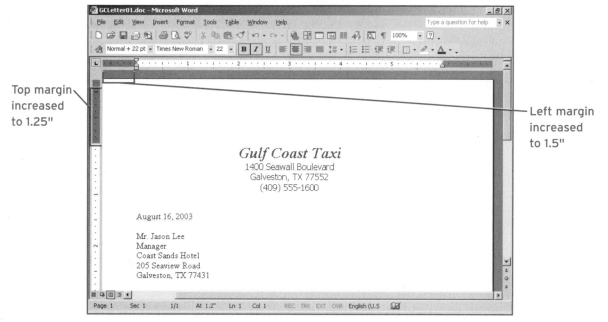

Top margin increased to 1.25"

Left margin increased to 1.5"

Skill Set 3
Formatting Documents

Modify Document Layout and Page Setup Options
Modify Page Orientation

Most documents are meant to be printed lengthwise on a page. This is called **portrait** orientation. Some documents look best if they are printed sideways on the page. This is called **landscape** orientation. The default for Word documents is portrait, but you can change the orientation to landscape in the Page Setup dialog box.

To set different orientations in a document, select the text to which you want to apply the new orientation, open the Margins tab in the Page Setup dialog box, select the orientation, then click Selected text in the Apply to list.

Activity Steps

open GCAnnouncement01.doc

1. Click the **Zoom button list arrow** 100%, then click **Whole Page** to see the entire page in portrait orientation
2. Click **File** on the menu bar, then click **Page Setup** to open the Page Setup dialog box
3. Click the **Margins tab**, if necessary
4. Click the **Landscape orientation box**
   See Figure 3-19.
5. Click **OK**
   See Figure 3-20.

close GCAnnouncement01.doc

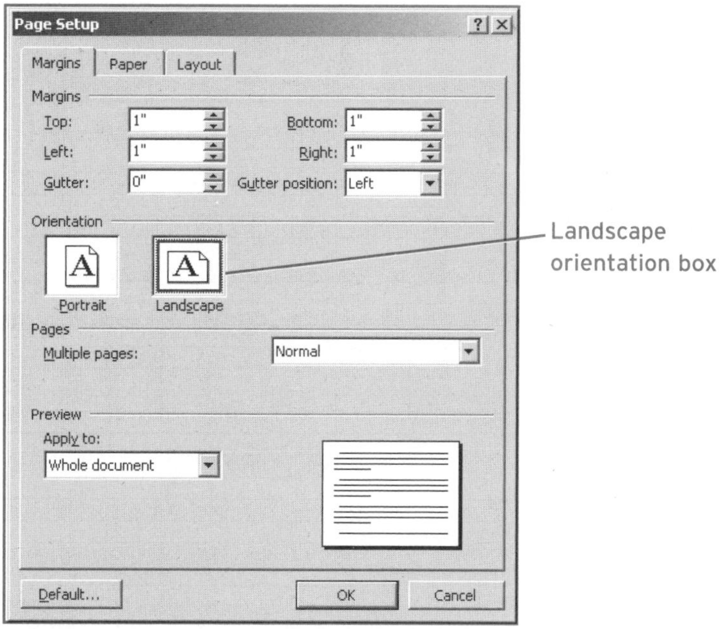

Figure 3-19: Margins tab in Page Setup dialog box

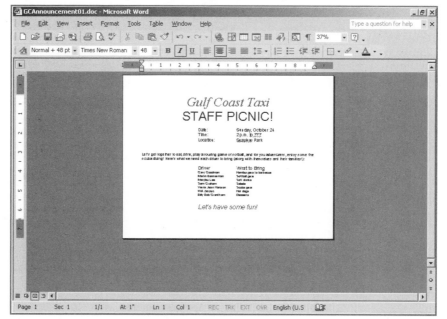

Landscape orientation box

Figure 3-20: Document in landscape orientation

Skill Set 3
Formatting Documents

Create and Modify Tables
Create Tables

You can use tabs to arrange text in rows and columns, but when you have a lot of information to present in that format, a table is usually a better choice. A table sets up a grid of rows and columns. Each intersection of a row and column is called a **cell**. To move from one cell to another, you press [Tab] or an arrow key.

Activity Steps

 open GCBrochure04.doc

1. Press **[Ctrl][End]** to position the insertion point at the end of the document, then press **[Enter]**

2. Click the **Insert Table button**

3. Move the pointer over the grid to create a **4 × 3 Table**
   See Figure 3-21.

4. Click to create the table

5. Type **Destination**, press **[Tab]**, type **Average Time**, press **[Tab]**, type **Average Fare**, then press **[Tab]**

6. Type the rest of the information in the table as shown in Figure 3-22 in the same manner

 close GCBrochure04.doc

Step 6
If you press [Tab] after the last entry and accidentally insert a new row, click the Undo button.

Figure 3-21: Using the Table button

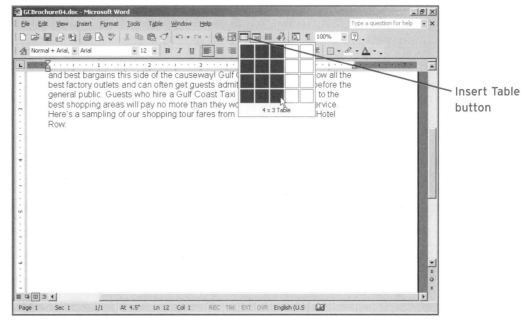

Insert Table button

Figure 3-22: Completed table

Tables and Borders toolbar may not appear on your screen

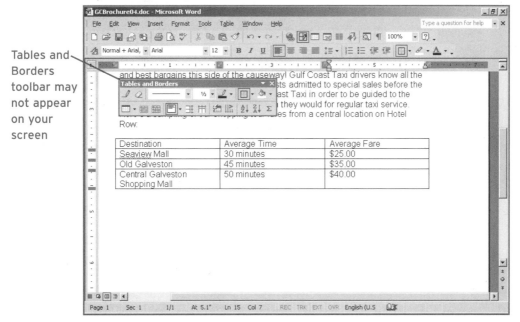

Skill Set 3
Formatting Documents

Create and Modify Tables
Modify Tables

Once you have created a table, you can modify it in several ways. You can resize the table to fit better on the page. You can merge several cells to form one cell, or you can split one cell to form several cells. You can also rotate text in a cell. These are only a few of the changes you can make to a table.

To make several columns or rows the same size, select them, then click the Distribute Columns Evenly button or the Distribute Rows Evenly button on the Tables and Borders toolbar.

Activity Steps

 open GCBrochure05.doc

1. Scroll down until you can see the table, then move the pointer anywhere over the table to see the table move and resize handles *See Figure 3-23.*

2. Position the pointer over the **table resize handle** ⊞ so that the pointer changes to ⊞, then drag the resize handle to the left until the dotted outline indicates that the table is approximately 4.5" wide

3. Drag the **table move handle** ⊞ to center the table horizontally on the page

4. If the Tables and Borders toolbar is not open, right-click any toolbar, then click **Tables and Borders**

5. Position the pointer over the first column so that the pointer changes to ↓, then click to select the entire first column

6. Click the **Merge Cells button** ▦ on the Tables and Borders toolbar

7. With the first column still selected, click the **Change Text Direction button** ▥ twice to rotate the text to read vertically up the page, then click anywhere in the table to deselect the text *See Figure 3-24.*

8. Click the **Close button** ✕ on the Tables and Borders toolbar

 close GCBrochure05.doc

Figure 3-23: Table handles

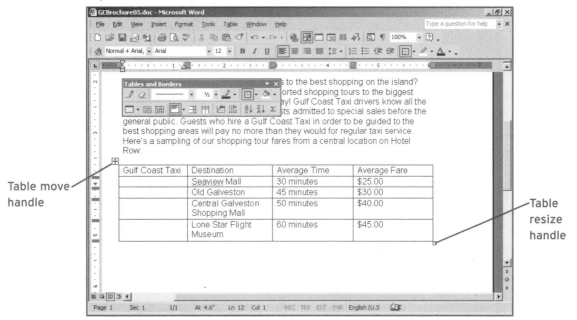

Table move handle

Table resize handle

Figure 3-24: Modified table

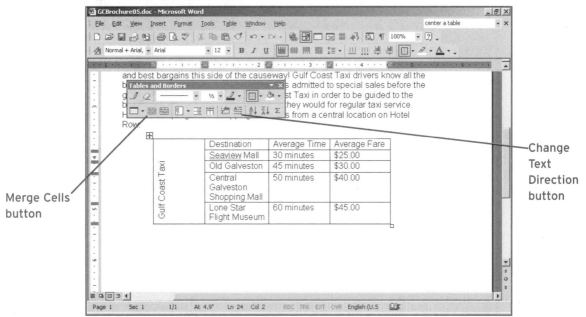

Merge Cells button

Change Text Direction button

Skill Set 3
Formatting Documents

Create and Modify Tables
Apply AutoFormat to Tables

After you create a table, you can format it to make it look better. The quickest way to format a table is to use the Table AutoFormat command on the Table menu.

Activity Steps

 open GCMemo03.doc

1. Scroll down until you can see the table, then click anywhere within the table
2. Right-click any toolbar, then click **Tables and Borders** to open the Tables and Borders toolbar, if necessary
3. Click the **Table AutoFormat button** on the Tables and Borders toolbar to open the Table AutoFormat dialog box
4. Scroll up the Table styles list, then click **Table Classic 3**
5. Click the **Last row** and **Last column check boxes** to deselect them
   See Figure 3-25.
6. Click **Apply**
7. Click the **table move handle** to select the entire table, click the **Center button** to center the table on the page, then click anywhere in the document to deselect the table
   See Figure 3-26.
8. Click the **Close button** on the Tables and Borders toolbar

 close GCMemo03.doc

Step 7
You can drag the table move handle to position the table anywhere you like.

Figure 3-25: Table AutoFormat dialog box

Select check boxes to apply special formatting

Figure 3-26: Table with AutoFormat applied

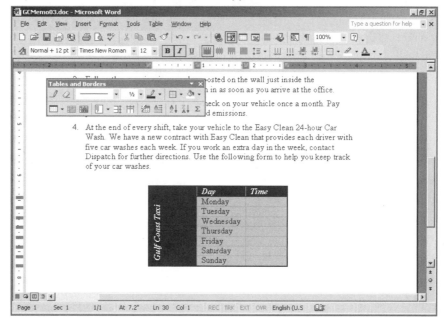

Skill Set 3

Formatting Documents

Create and Modify Tables
Modify Table Borders and Shading

You can manually change table borders and the shading in cells by changing the options in the Borders and Shading dialog box. You can make changes to these properties even after you've applied a table AutoFormat.

Activity Steps

 open GCBrochure06.doc

1. Scroll down until you can see the table, right-click any toolbar, then click **Tables and Borders** to open the Tables and Borders toolbar, if necessary

2. Move the pointer into the left margin to the left of the top row of the table so that it changes to , then click to select the top row
   See Figure 3-27.

Make sure the Line Style button displays the line style you want before you click one of the Borders buttons or draw a border.

3. Click the **Shading Color button list arrow** ⬛▾ on the Tables and Borders toolbar, then click the **Blue box**

4. Select the bottom four rows in the table, click the **Shading color button list arrow** ⬛▾ on the Tables and Borders toolbar, then click the **Light Turquoise box**

5. Click the **Outside Border button list arrow** ⬛▾ on the Tables and Borders toolbar, click the **All Borders button** ⊞, then click anywhere in the table to deselect the text

6. Click the **Line Style button list arrow** |——————▾| on the Tables and Borders toolbar, then click the thick line with thin lines above and below it

7. Drag the pointer, which changes to ✏, across the line below the top row, then click the **Draw Table button** ✏ on the Tables and Borders toolbar to deselect it
   See Figure 3-28.

8. Click the **Close button** ✕ on the Tables and Borders toolbar

 close GCBrochure06.doc

Figure 3-27: Selecting a row in a table

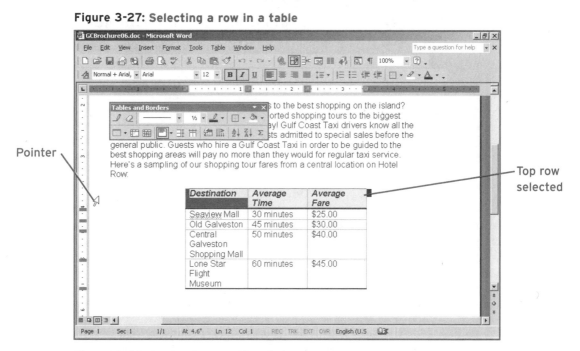

Pointer

Top row selected

Figure 3-28: Table with modified borders and shading

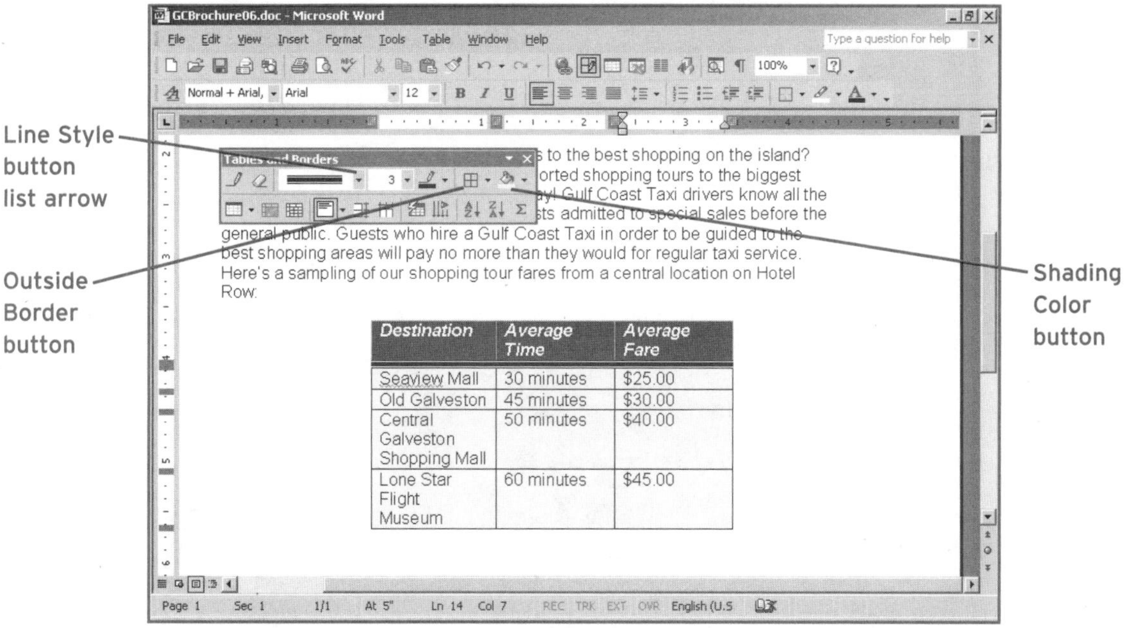

Line Style button list arrow

Outside Border button

Shading Color button

Create and Modify Tables
Insert and Delete Columns and Rows in a Table

You can add additional columns and rows to a table by using the Insert command on the Table menu. You can delete extra columns and rows from a table by using the Delete command on the Table menu.

If you want to prevent a table that flows onto a second page from breaking in the middle of a row, position the insertion point in the table, click Table Properties on the Table menu, click the Row tab, then click the Allow row to break across pages check box to deselect it.

Activity Steps

 open GCMemo04.doc

1. Scroll down so you can see the entire table, then click anywhere in the **Weekly Hours column**

2. Click **Table** on the menu bar, point to **Insert**, then click **Columns to the Right** to insert a new column to the right of the current column

3. Select the row with **Gary Goodman** in the **Driver column**

4. Click **Table** on the menu bar, point to **Insert**, then click **Rows Above** to insert a row above the selected row
   See Figure 3-29.

5. Select the row with **Verna Graham** in the **Driver column**

6. Right-click the selected row, then click **Delete Rows** on the shortcut menu
   See Figure 3-30.

close GCMemo04.doc

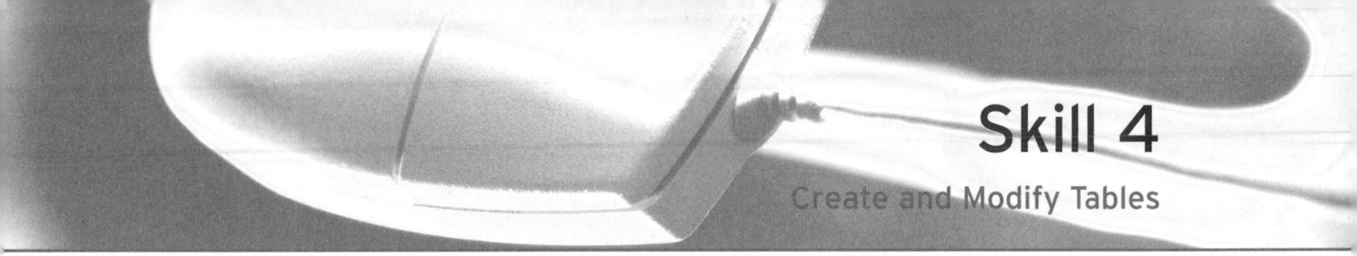

Figure 3-29: Column and row inserted in table

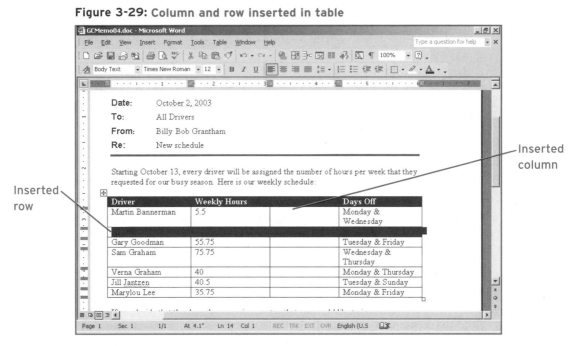

Inserted column

Inserted row

Figure 3-30: Table with row deleted

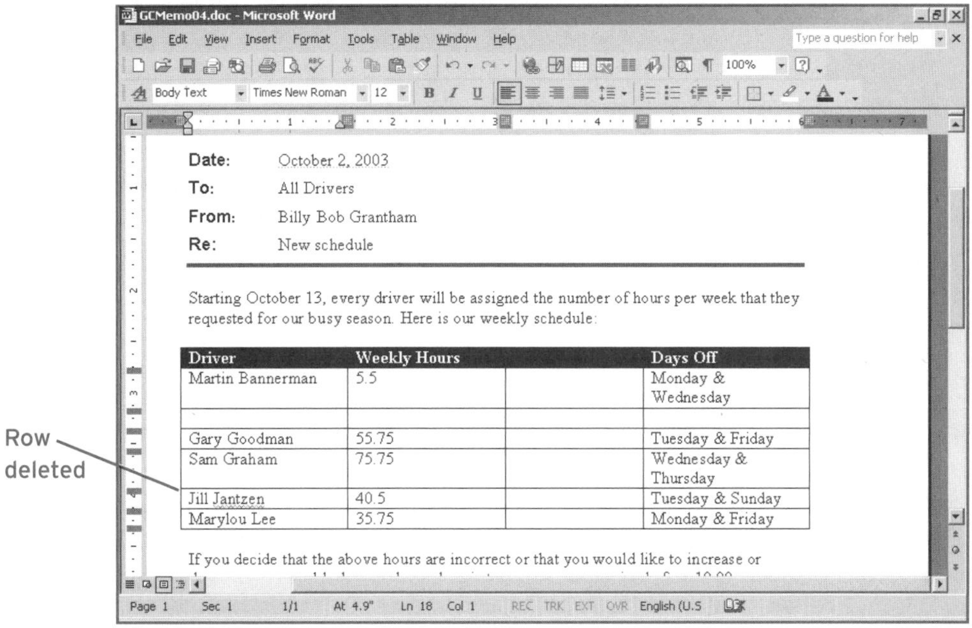

Row deleted

Skill Set 3

Formatting Documents

Create and Modify Tables
Modify Cell Format in a Table

You can format the text in cells just as you format regular text. For example, you can change the alignment of text within a cell, or you can add additional blank space around the entry in a cell.

To repeat the heading rows of a table automatically if a table occupies more than one page, select the header row (or rows), click Table, then click Heading Rows Repeat.

Activity Steps

 open GCMemo05.doc

1. Scroll down until you can see the table, right-click any toolbar, then click **Tables and Borders** to open the Tables and Borders toolbar, if necessary

2. Drag to select all of the cells except those in the top row, then click the **Align Top Left button list arrow** on the Tables and Borders toolbar

3. Click the **Align Center Left button**

4. Click **Table** on the menu bar, click **Table Properties**, then click the **Table tab**, if necessary

5. Click **Options** on the Table tab to open the Table Options dialog box

6. Click the **Top up arrow** six times to change the Top cell margin to **0.06"**, then change the Bottom cell margin to **0.06"**
   See Figure 3-31.

7. Click **OK**, click **OK** in the Table Properties dialog box, then click anywhere on the screen to deselect the cells
   See Figure 3-32.

8. Click the **Close button** on the Tables and Borders toolbar

 close GCMemo05.doc

Figure 3-31: Table Options dialog box

Cell margins ———

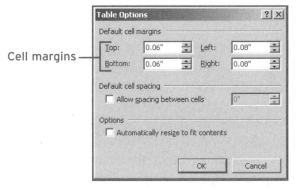

Figure 3-32: Table with modified cell formats

Increased
space above
and below
text in cells

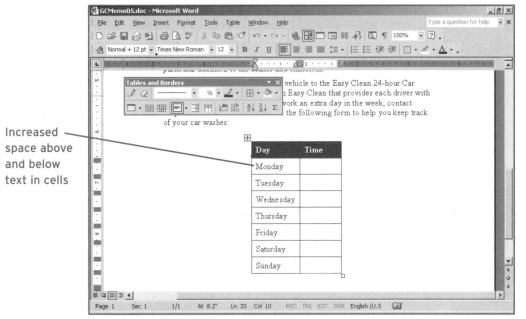

Skill Set 3
Formatting Documents

Preview and Print Documents, Envelopes, and Labels
Preview a Document

Before you print a document, you should look at it in Print Preview to make sure that it will print the way you expect it to.

You can print from Print Preview by clicking the Print button or using the Print command on the File menu.

Activity Steps

 open GCLetter02.doc

1. Click the **Print Preview button** 🔍
2. Click below the scroll box in the vertical scroll bar to move to the second page
3. Position the pointer over the page so that it changes to 🔍, click the line of text on page 2 to zoom in, and observe that the pointer changes to 🔍
   See Figure 3-33.
4. Click the screen again to zoom back out
5. Click the **Shrink to Fit button** 🔲 on the Print Preview toolbar
   See Figure 3-34.
6. Click the **Close button** on the Print Preview toolbar

 close GCLetter02.doc

---

extra!

Adjusting text in Print Preview
You can enter and edit text in Print Preview. Click the Magnifier button 🔍 on the Print Preview toolbar to deselect it and change the pointer to I. Click the screen at the point where you want to insert or edit text, then start typing. When you are finished editing, click the Magnifier button again, and the pointer changes back to 🔍 or 🔍.

Certification Circle

Figure 3-33: Document magnified in Print Preview

Pointer

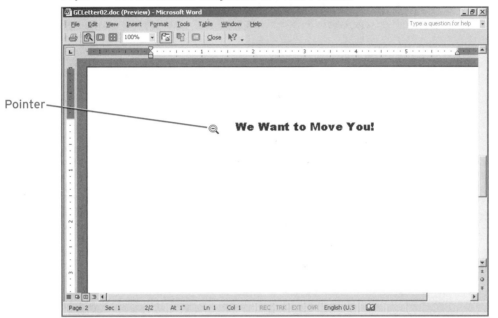

Figure 3-34: Text shrunk to fit on one page in Print Preview

Shrink to
Fit button

Pointer

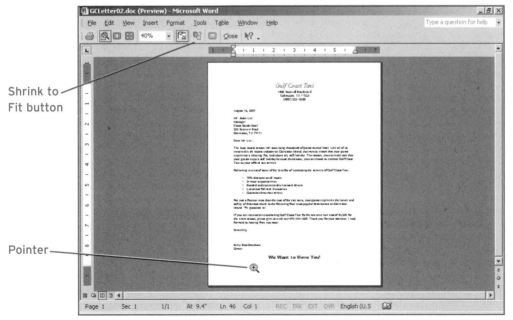

Skill Set 3

Formatting Documents

Preview and Print Documents, Envelopes, and Labels

Print a Document

Once you've created a document, you usually want to print it. To print a document, you can click the Print command on the File menu to change print settings (like the number of copies to print), or you can click the Print button to print your document with the current print settings.

When you click the Print button, the Print dialog box does not open, and the document prints using the current print settings.

Activity Steps

 open GCProposal03.doc

1. Click **File** on the menu bar, then click **Print** to open the Print dialog box

2. Click the **Pages option button**, then type **2-3** to print only the last two pages

3. Click the **Number of copies up arrow** to change the number of copies to **2**

4. Make sure the **Collate check box** is selected
   See Figure 3-35.

5. Click **OK**

 close GCProposal03.doc

Figure 3-35: Print dialog box

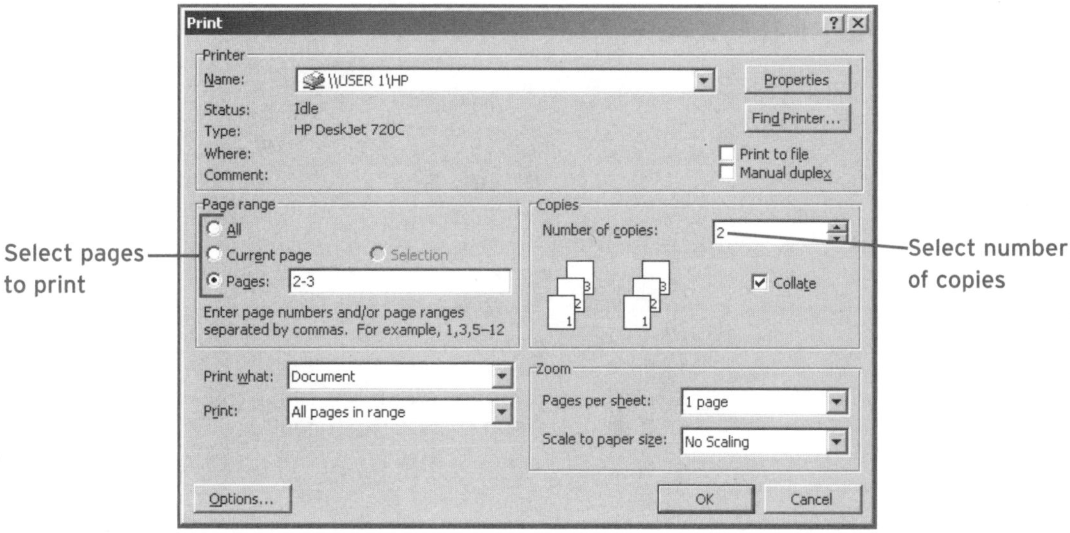

Select pages to print →

Select number ← of copies

extra!

Print dialog box options

To change your printer's options, click Properties at the top of the Print dialog box. To print several document pages on one piece of paper, select one of the options from the Pages per sheet list in the Print dialog box. To scale the document to fit on a specific paper size, click the Scale to paper size list arrow in the Print dialog box.

Skill Set 3
Formatting Documents

Preview and Print Documents, Envelopes, and Labels
Print Envelopes

You can set up a document to print as an envelope. With the Envelopes and Labels command, you simply type the address, tell Word what size envelope you are using, and Word formats the address to fit in the proper position on the envelope. After you create your envelope, you can print it directly from the Envelopes and Labels dialog box, or you can click Add to Document to add it to the current document as a new section.

Activity Steps

 open GCLetter03.doc

1. Click **Tools** on the menu bar, point to **Letters and Mailings**, click **Envelopes and Labels**, then click the **Envelopes tab**, if necessary

2. Make sure that the Delivery address is the address for **Anna Perkins**, as shown in the letter
   See Figure 3-36.

3. Click in the **Return address box**, type **Gulf Coast Taxi**, press **[Enter]**, type **1400 Seawall Blvd.**, press **[Enter]**, then type **Galveston, TX 77552**

4. Click the **Feed box** to open the Printing Options tab in the Envelope Options dialog box, note the selected direction to feed the envelope into the printer, then click **OK**

5. Click the **Preview box** to open the Envelope Options tab in the Envelope Options dialog box, click the **Envelope size list arrow**, read through the list of envelope sizes, make sure that **Size 10** (the standard business size envelope) is selected in the list, then click **OK**

6. Click **Add to Document** to add the envelope as a new section in the current document, then if necessary, click **No** in the dialog box that opens asking if you want to save the return address as the default return address

7. Click the **Print Preview button**
   See Figure 3-37.

8. Click below the scroll box in the vertical scroll bar to move to the second page

9. Click **File** on the menu bar, click **Print**, click the **Pages option button**, type **1**, insert your envelope into the printer, then click **OK**

   close GCLetter03.doc

Step 2
You can change the Delivery address from the one suggested by typing a different one or by clicking the Insert Address button to insert a name and address from your electronic address book.

Figure 3-36: Envelopes tab in the Envelopes and Labels dialog box

Delivery address picked up from inside address in letter

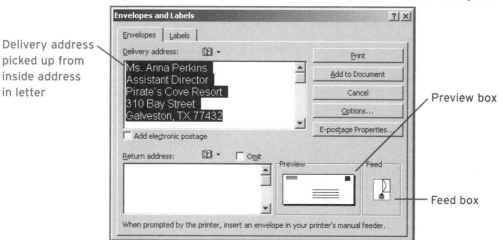

Preview box

Feed box

Figure 3-37: Envelope in Print Preview

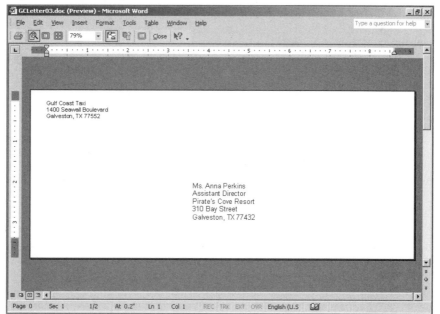

Skill Set 3
Formatting Documents

Preview and Print Documents, Envelopes, and Labels
Printing Labels

Labels are as easy to print as envelopes. Click the Labels tab in the Envelopes and Labels dialog box and select the options for the size of labels you are using. Word automatically formats the address to fit on the labels. After you create your label, you can print it directly from the Envelopes and Labels dialog box, or you can click New Document to create a new document so you can see how the labels will print.

Step 5
If your label is not in the Product number list in the Label Options dialog box, click New Label and specify the dimensions of your label.

Activity Steps

1. Open a new, blank document

2. Click **Tools** on the menu bar, point to **Letters and Mailings**, click **Envelopes and Labels**, then click the **Labels tab** if necessary

3. Click in the **Address box**, type **Mr. Jason Lee**, press **[Enter]**, then continue typing the address in the Address box, as shown in Figure 3-38

4. Click the **Label box** to open the Label Options dialog box, then examine the list of labels in the Product number list

5. Click the label that you are using in the Product number list (if you do not have a label, choose any label in the list), then click **OK**

6. Click **New Document**, click the **Zoom button list arrow** 100% ▾ , then click **Whole Page**
   See Figure 3-39.

7. Click the **Print button** 🖨

   close file

Figure 3-38: Labels tab in Envelopes and Labels dialog box

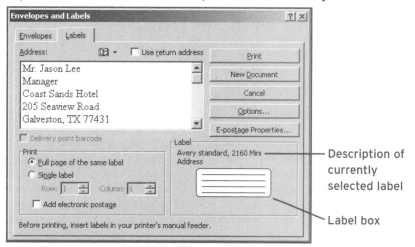

Description of currently selected label

Label box

Figure 3-39: Labels in document

Temporary filename

Your layout may look different depending on the label you chose

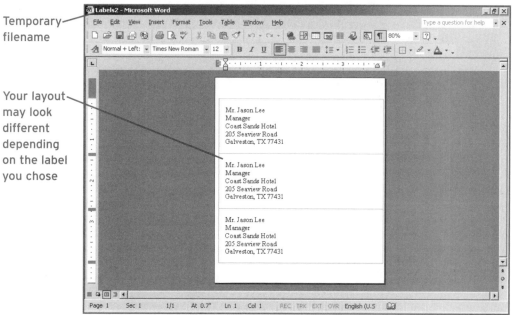

Skill Set 3
Formatting Documents

Targeting Your Skills

1 Create the document shown in Figure 3-40. Insert a footer that identifies the page number and the total number of pages. Position this text so it is on the right side of the footer. Finally, make sure the columns are balanced. Preview your completed document and print it.

Figure 3-40

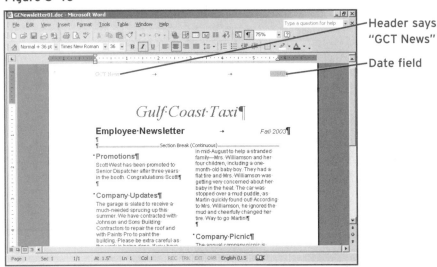

Header says "GCT News"

Date field

2 Create the document shown in Figure 3-41. Note that you need to insert page numbers and change the margins. Preview your completed document and print it.

Figure 3-41

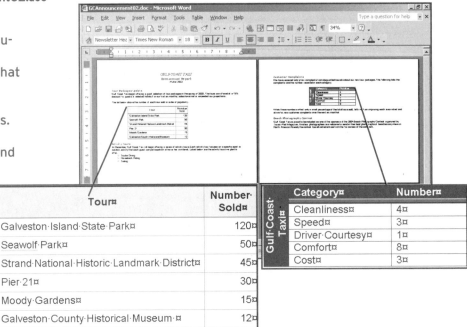

Tour¤	Number·Sold¤
Galveston·Island·State·Park¤	120¤
Seawolf·Park¤	50¤
Strand·National·Historic·Landmark·District¤	45¤
Pier·21¤	30¤
Moody·Gardens¤	15¤
Galveston·County·Historical·Museum·¤	12¤

Category¤	Number¤
Cleanliness¤	4¤
Speed¤	3¤
Driver·Courtesy¤	1¤
Comfort¤	8¤
Cost¤	3¤

Skill List

1. Manage files and folders for documents
2. Create documents using templates
3. Save documents using different names and file formats

In Skill Set 4, you will learn about managing documents. First, you will learn how to create folders within Word. Folders make it easy to organize your files so that you can quickly locate them when you want them. Then you will learn how to create a document from a template, which is a pre-designed document. Finally, you will learn how to save your documents with different names and in different file formats.

Learning how to manage your documents will save you time. If you master these skills, you will always be able to locate, organize, and store your documents quickly.

Skill Set 4

Managing Documents

Manage Files and Folders for Documents

Using the Open and Save As dialog boxes in Word, you can create new folders. To create a new folder, you click the Create New Folder button in the dialog box, then type a name for the folder. The folder is created as a new folder within the current folder, and the new folder becomes the current folder. Specifically, the Look in box at the top of the Open dialog box or the Save in box at the top of the Save As dialog box changes to display the new folder name.

Step 3
The Create New Folder button is also available on the toolbar at the top of the Open dialog box.

Activity Steps

1. Create a new, blank document

2. Click **File** on the menu bar, then click **Save As** to open the Save As dialog box

3. Click the **Create New Folder button** 🖿 on the toolbar at the top of the Open dialog box

4. Type **My New Folder** in the Name box

5. Click **OK**
   See Figure 4-1.

6. Click the **Up One Level button** 🖻 on the toolbar at the top of the Save As dialog box to see your new folder in the folder list
   See Figure 4-2.

7. Click **Cancel** to close the Save As dialog box without saving the file

 close file

Figure 4-1: New folder created in Save As dialog box

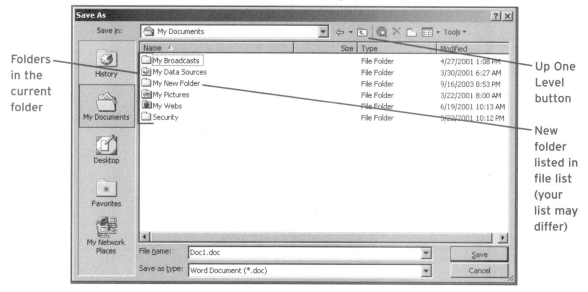

Current folder

Create New Folder button

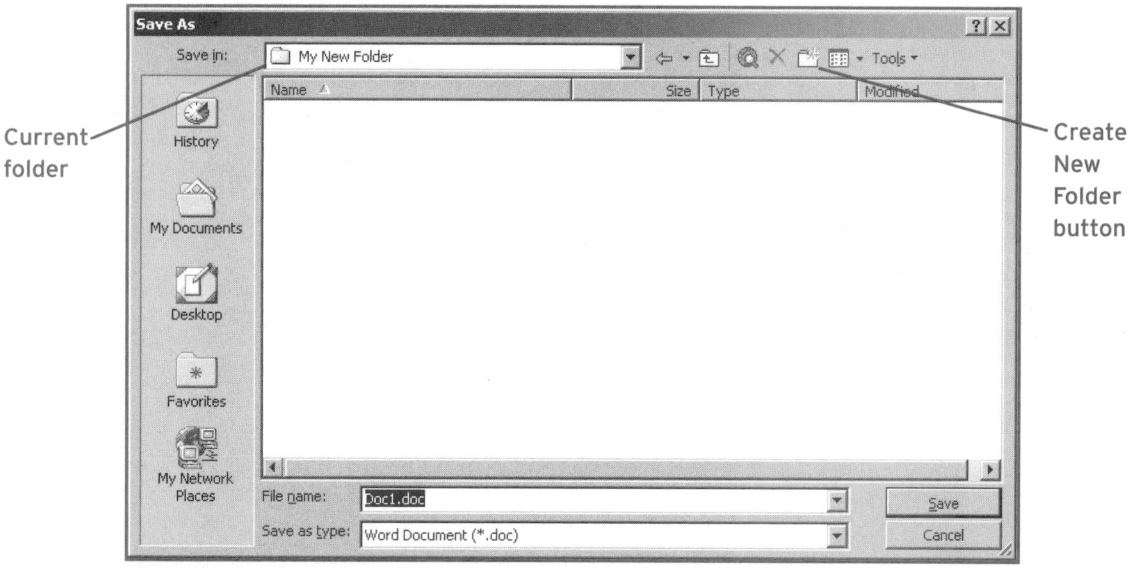

Figure 4-2: New folder listed in Save As dialog box

Folders in the current folder

Up One Level button

New folder listed in file list (your list may differ)

Skill Set 4

Managing Documents

Create Documents Using Templates

A **template** is a set of styles and formats that determines how a document will look. Every document is based on the Normal template, a template that is available to all documents. Word provides additional templates to make it easier for you to create specially formatted documents, like memos and resumes. Most templates provided with Word include **placeholders**, items you click once to select all of the existing text, then type to substitute your replacement text. When you save a document created from a template, it is saved as an ordinary Word document.

To use any existing document as a template for a new document, click the Choose document link in the New Document task pane to open a copy of the document.

Activity Steps

1. If the task pane is not open, click **View** on the menu bar, then click **Task Pane**

2. If the New Document task pane is not visible, click the **Other Task Panes list arrow** in the task pane title bar, then click **New Document**

3. Click the **General Templates link** in the New Document task pane to open the Templates dialog box

4. Click the **Other Documents tab**, click **Contemporary Resume**, then make sure that the **Document option button** is selected under Create New
   See Figure 4-3.

5. Click **OK**

6. Click the **[Click here and type address] placeholder**, type **4598 Main Street**, press [Enter], then type **Charleston, SC 29407**

7. Drag to select the name **Deborah Greer**, then type **Mark Rodriguez**
   See Figure 4-4.

 close file

Figure 4-3: Templates dialog box

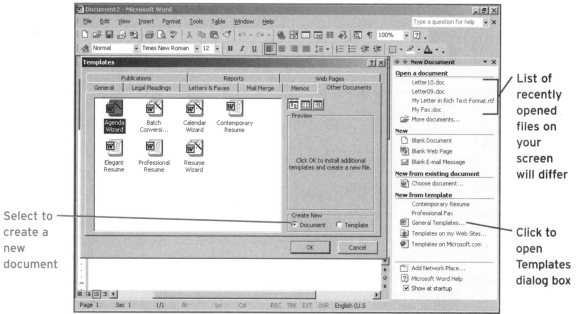

Select to create a new document

List of recently opened files on your screen will differ

Click to open Templates dialog box

Figure 4-4: Resume template with text selected

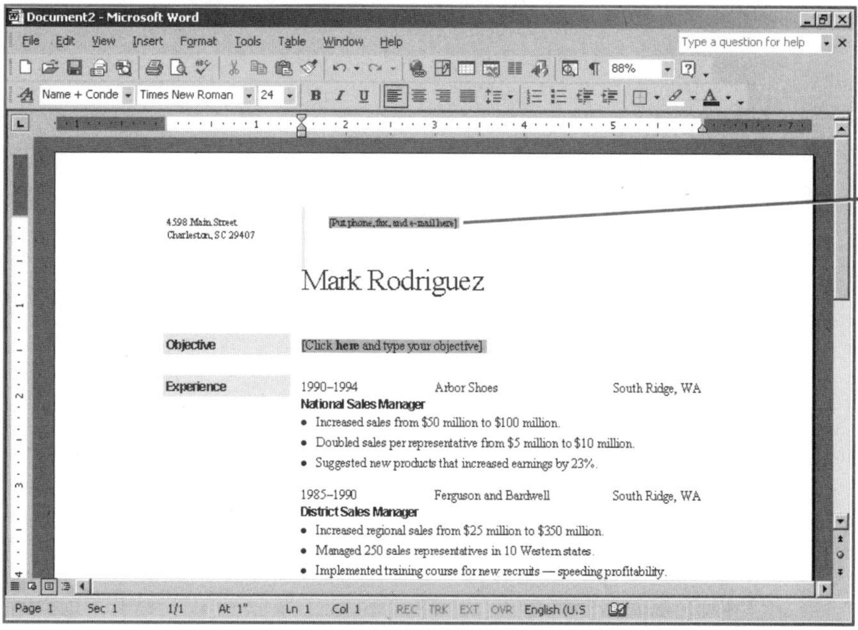

Placeholder

Skill Set 4
Managing Documents

Save Documents Using Different Names and File Formats
Save a Document

When you create a new document, you will probably need to save it. When you save a new document for the first time, you use the Save As dialog box, where you can change the drive and folder to which you are saving the file and specify the filename. If you want to save a copy of the document with a new name, you use the Save As command. If you make changes to a document and then want to save the changes without creating a new copy of the document, you use the Save command.

Step 3
If you want to save your document to the My Documents folder, you can click My Documents in the Places bar on the left in the Save As dialog box.

Activity Steps

 open EWLetter09.doc

1. Click **File** on the menu bar, then click **Save As**
2. Type **My Saved Letter** in the File name box
3. Click the **Save in list arrow**, then select the folder or drive to which you want to save your document
4. Double-click the folder name in which you want to save your document
   See Figure 4-5.
5. Click **Save** in the Save As dialog box
   See Figure 4-6.
6. Select **August 15** in the first paragraph in the body of the letter, then type **September 8**
7. Click the **Save button** 🖫 to save the change to the document

 close My Saved Letter.doc

Figure 4-5: Save As dialog box

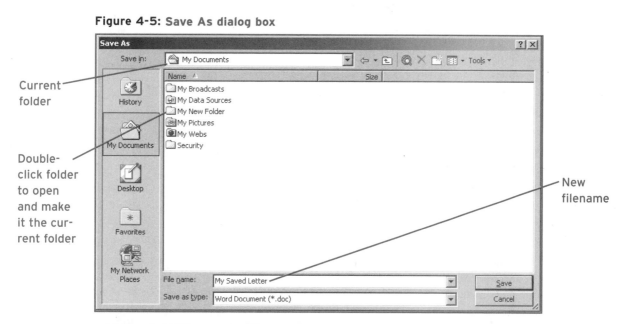

Current folder

Double-click folder to open and make it the current folder

New filename

Figure 4-6: File saved with a new name

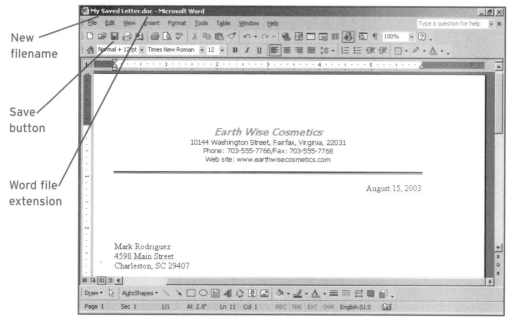

New filename

Save button

Word file extension

Earth Wise Cosmetics
10144 Washington Street, Fairfax, Virginia, 22031
Phone: 703-555-7766/Fax: 703-555-7768
Web site: www.earthwisecosmetics.com

August 15, 2003

Mark Rodriguez
4598 Main Street
Charleston, SC 29407

Skill Set 4
Managing Documents

Save Documents Using Different Names and File Formats
Save a Document with a Different File Format

When you save a document, you save it in the default Word file format. The file extension is .doc. If you are sending the file to someone who doesn't have Word, you can save the file with a different file format. For example, rich text format is a format that most word processors can read and will allow you to save most of your formatting. To save a document with a different file format, you need to use the Save As command.

Step 3
Select the file type Document Templates (*.dot) to save the file as a Word template that appears on the General tab in the Templates dialog box.

Activity Steps

 open EWMemo07.doc

1. Click **File** on the menu bar, then click **Save As** to open the Save As dialog box
2. Type **My Memo in Rich Text Format** in the File name box
3. Click the **Save as type list arrow**, then click **Rich Text Format (*.rtf)**
4. Click the **Save in list arrow**, then select the folder or drive to which you want to save your document
   See Figure 4-7.
5. Click **Save** in the Save As dialog box
   See Figure 4-8.

 close My Memo in Rich Text Format.rtf

Figure 4-7: Save As dialog box with Rich Text Format selected

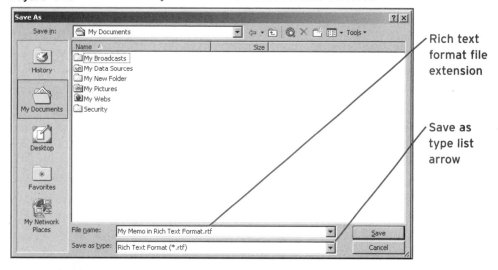

Rich text format file extension

Save as type list arrow

Figure 4-8: File saved in rich text format

Rich text format file extension

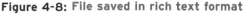

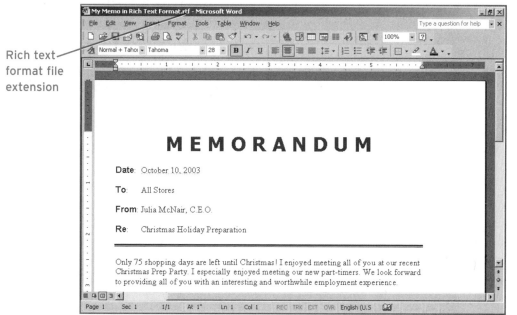

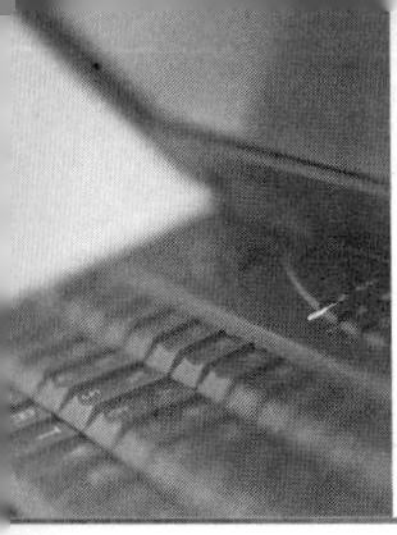

Skill Set 4

Managing Documents

Target Your Skills

EWNewsletter06.doc

1 Use Figure 4-9 as a guide to save the EWNewsletter06 file with a new name as a template. Make sure you save it in the folder indicated (you'll need to create the folder first).

Figure 4-9

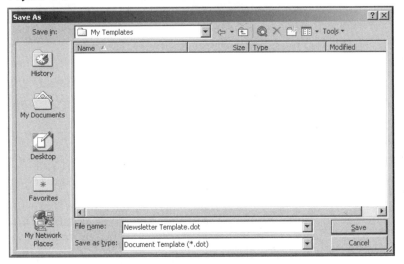

2 Use Figure 4-10 as a guide for creating a fax cover sheet from the Professional Fax template. (*Hint*: To insert a checkmark in a box, double-click the box. To delete the **Company Name Here** box, position the pointer above it so that it looks like a downward-pointing arrow, click to select the entire box, then click the Cut button.) Save the file as **My Fax**.

Figure 4-10

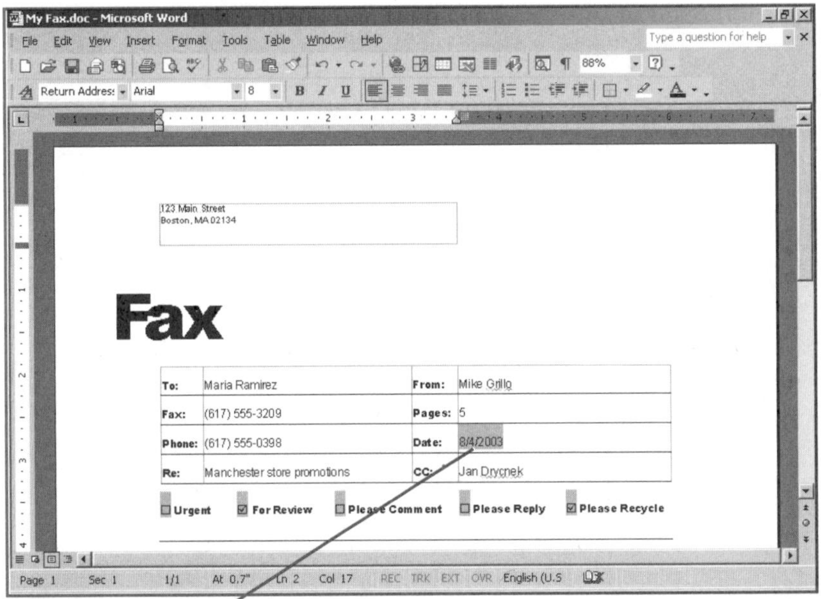

Current date will appear here

Skill List

1. Insert images and graphics
2. Create and modify diagrams and charts

Pictures, diagrams, and charts can make your documents more interesting and informative. For example, you might want to insert a company logo or an image into a newsletter. You can insert clip art or other pictures stored on your hard drive or on the Web.

You can use the Insert Diagram command to insert a variety of diagrams, including an organizational chart diagram or a pyramid diagram. Diagrams can help get your point across visually. You can also use a program built into Word called Microsoft Graph to insert a graph of numerical data.

Skill Set 5
Working with Graphics

Insert Images and Graphics
Insert Clips Using the Clip Organizer

A **clip**, sometimes called **clip art**, is a drawing, photograph, sound, or movie that you can insert into a document. Clips are organized in the Clip Organizer in collections, or groups on the basis of keywords stored with the file. You can find clips appropriate to your subject by searching for a keyword you type in the Insert Clip Art task pane.

Activity Steps

 open GCAnnouncement03.doc

1. If the Drawing toolbar is not visible, click the **Drawing button** 🖉, then position the insertion point between the headline and the paragraph

2. Click the **Insert Clip Art button** 🖫 on the Drawing toolbar to open the Insert Clip Art task pane

3. If a dialog box appears asking if you want to catalog your clips, click **Later**

4. Click in the **Search text box** in the task pane, if necessary delete any text that is already there (from a previous search), type **wedding**, then click **Search**

5. Click the **clip** indicated in Figure 5-1 (if you don't have this clip, select another), then click the **Close button** ☒ in the Insert Clip Art task pane

6. Click the clip to select it, then drag the **lower-right sizing handle** down and to the right until the dotted outline indicates that the clip extends to the right margin of the paragraph as shown in Figure 5-2

7. Click anywhere in a blank area of the document to deselect the clip

 close GCAnnouncement03.doc

To add your own clips to the Clip Organizer, on the File menu in the Clip Organizer, point to Add Clips to Gallery, click On My Own, click the clip you want to add, click Add to, click the collection in which you want to store the clip, then click Add.

Browsing the Clip Organizer
Click the Clip Organizer link at the bottom of the Insert Clip Art task pane to open the Microsoft Clip Organizer. You can click the various folders in the Collection List on the left to see the contents of each category. If there is a plus sign next to a folder, click it to see the list of folders within that folder. To insert clips into a document from the Clip Organizer, simply drag the clip to your document.

Figure 5-1: Insert Clip Art task pane

Select this clip

Figure 5-2: Resizing a clip

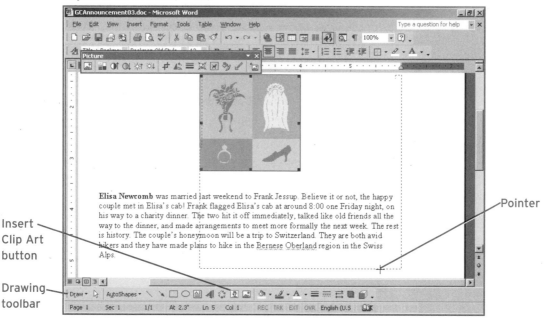

Pointer

Insert
Clip Art
button

Drawing
toolbar

Skill Set 5

Working with Graphics

Insert Images and Graphics
Insert Images Not Stored in the Clip Organizer

In addition to clips from the Clip Organizer, you can insert graphic images stored on your hard drive, another disk, or on the Web. Graphic images are saved in many file formats. Common file formats for graphics include .bmp, .tif, .jgp (also called JPEG), and .wmf.

Activity Steps

 open GCProposal04.doc

1. If the Drawing toolbar is not visible, click the **Drawing button** 🖉, click the **Zoom button list arrow** `100%`, then click **Whole Page**

2. With the insertion point at the beginning of the document, click the **Insert Picture button** 🖾 on the Drawing toolbar to open the Insert Picture dialog box

3. Locate the **GCTaxiLogo01.bmp** project file, then click it to select it *See Figure 5-3.*

4. Click **Insert** to insert the image at the insertion point

5. Click the image to select it, then drag the **bottom-right sizing handle** down and to the right until the dotted line indicates that the right edge of the image will be aligned with the **T** in **Taxi**

6. With the image still selected, click the **Center button** ▦

7. Click anywhere in the document to deselect the image *See Figure 5-4.*

 close GCProposal04.doc

tip

To insert a picture directly from a scanner or a digital camera, point to Picture on the Insert menu, then click From Scanner or Camera.

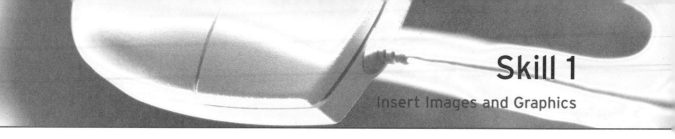

Figure 5-3: Logo selected in the Insert Picture dialog box

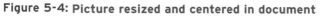

Figure 5-4: Picture resized and centered in document

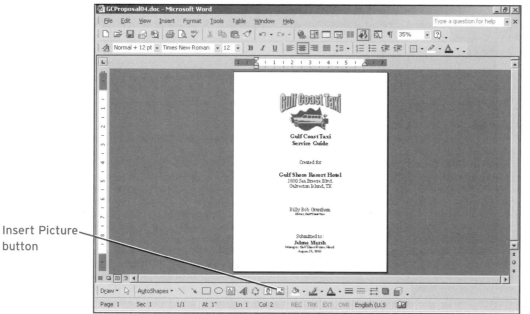

Insert Picture button

Skill Set 5

Working with Graphics

Create and Modify Diagrams and Charts
Create an Organizational Chart

Sometimes diagrams can convey information more clearly than a written description. You can insert a variety of diagrams into a Word document using the Insert Diagram or Organization Chart button. An **organizational chart** is a graphical representation of a hierarchical structure.

Right-click the edge of a chart box to see commands you can use to format or change the organizational chart.

Activity Steps

1. Open a new, blank document, then, if the Drawing toolbar is not visible, click the **Drawing button**

2. Click the **Insert Diagram or Organization Chart button** on the Drawing toolbar to open the Diagram Gallery dialog box

3. Make sure the **Organization Chart button** is selected
   See Figure 5-5.

4. Click **OK** to insert an organizational chart into the document

5. Click in the top box in the chart, type **Billy Bob Grantham**, press [Enter], type **Owner**, then click outside the box but inside the drawing canvas to automatically resize the box

6. Click in the first box on the left in the second row, type **Scott West**, press [Enter], then continue filling in the boxes as shown in Figure 5-6

    **close file**

Figure 5-5: Diagram Gallery dialog box

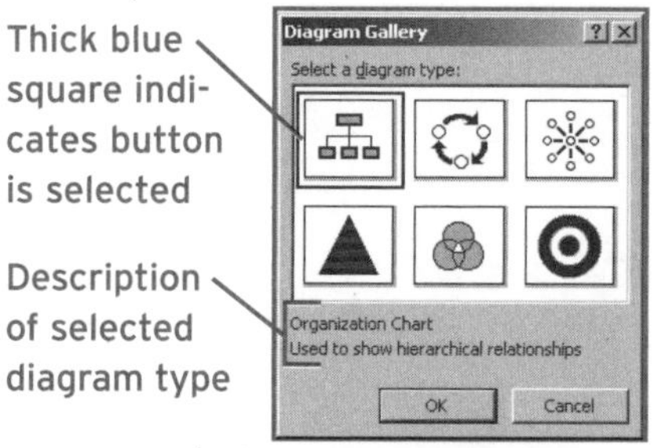

Thick blue square indicates button is selected

Description of selected diagram type

Figure 5-6: Completed organizational chart

Organization Chart toolbar

Drawing canvas

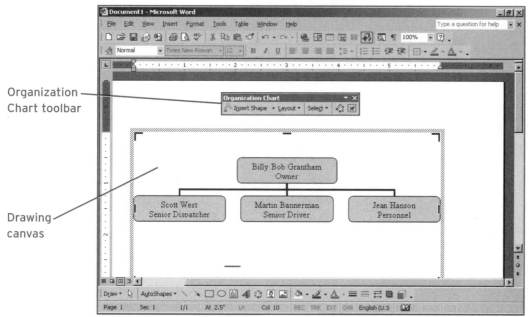

Skill Set 5

Working with Graphics

Create and Modify Diagrams and Charts
Modify an Organizational Chart

Once you have created a diagram or organizational chart, you can add elements to it and change their formatting. You can also rearrange the layout of the parts of the diagram.

Click the Layout button on the Organization Chart toolbar to change the arrangement of the boxes in the organizational chart.

Activity Steps

 open GCOrgChart01.doc

1. Click the **Jean Hanson box**, click the **Insert Shape button list arrow**  on the Organization Chart toolbar, click **Assistant**, click in the new Assistant box, then type **Mary Lou Lee**

2. Click the **Martin Bannerman box**, click the **Insert Shape button list arrow** , click **Subordinate**, then with the Martin Bannerman box still selected, add another Subordinate box

3. Click the edge of the **Mary Lou Lee box** with , then drag the box on top of the Scott West box

4. Click the edge of the **Subordinate box** on the left under the Martin Bannerman box, then press **[Delete]**
See Figure 5-7.

5. Click the **Autoformat button** on the Organization Chart toolbar, click **Beveled** in the list in the Organization Chart Style Gallery dialog box, then click **Apply**

6. Right-click the edge of one of the boxes, then click **Use AutoFormat** to turn off the AutoFormat option so you can add manual formats

7. If the Drawing toolbar is not visible, click the **Drawing button** , click the edge of the **Scott West box**, click the **Select button** on the Organization Chart toolbar, click **Level**, click the **Fill Color button list arrow** on the Drawing toolbar, then click the **Turquoise box**

8. Click the edge of the **Billy Bob Grantham box**, click the **Fill Color button list arrow** on the Drawing toolbar, click the **Blue box**, click the **Font Color button list arrow** , click the **White box**, click the **Bold button** , then click in a blank area of the document to deselect the chart and the drawing canvas (you may need to click twice)
See Figure 5-8.

 close GCOrgChart01.doc

Figure 5-7: Moving a box in an organizational chart

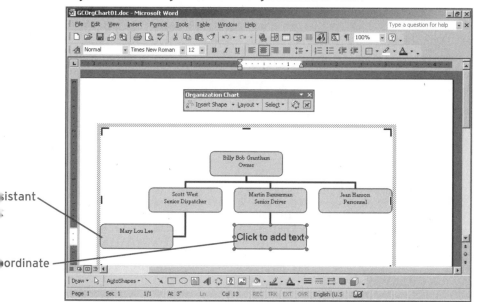

sistant

ordinate

Figure 5-8: Formatted organizational chart

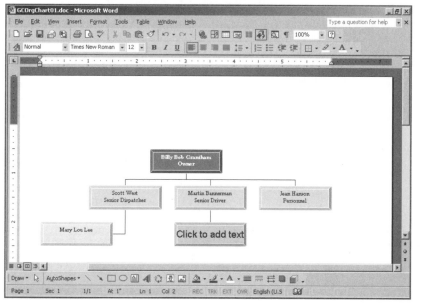

extra!

Understanding diagram types

In addition to organizational charts, you can create cycle, radial, pyramid, Venn, and target diagrams and flowcharts. Each diagram conveys information in a particular way by illustrating how a process works or by showing the relationship between parts of something larger. To create any of these diagrams except the flowchart, select the digram type in the Diagram Gallery dialog box. To create a flowchart, click the AutoShapes button on the Drawing toolbar, point to Flowchart, select the shape you want to insert, then drag to draw it in the document. Connect the flowchart shapes with lines from the Connectors or Lines categories on the AutoShapes menu.

Skill Set 5

Working with Graphics

Create and Modify Diagrams and Charts
Create a Chart

Graphs are a good way to communicate numerical information visually; for example, they can show at a glance how much sales have increased or whether one item is selling significantly more than another. You can add a graph to a document by using the built-in program Microsoft Graph. A graph consists of two parts: a **datasheet**, similar to a table or a spreadsheet, in which you enter the data you want to graph, and a **chart**, in which the data from the datasheet is graphed. When you start Microsoft Graph, the Word menu bar and toolbars are replaced with the Graph menu bar and toolbars.

Activity Steps

 open GCReport01.doc

1. Press **[Ctrl][End]** to position the insertion point at the end of the document, click **Insert** on the menu bar, then click **Object** to open the Object dialog box

2. Scroll down and click **Microsoft Graph Chart** in the Object type list, then click **OK**
   See Figure 5-9.

If the labels on an axis in the chart do not all appear, drag a sizing handle on the chart to enlarge the chart object while Microsoft Graph is still active.

3. Click the **1st Qtr cell**, type **Airport**, press **[Tab]**, type **Tours**, press **[Tab]**, then type **Shopping**

4. Double-click the **column D header** to eliminate this column from the chart

5. Click the **East cell**, type **October**, press **[Enter]**, type **November**, then double-click the **row 3 header** to eliminate this row from the chart

6. Click in the first cell below the Airport column heading, type **140**, then continue filling in the datasheet as shown in Figure 5-10

7. Drag the datasheet by its title bar so you can see the chart, then click anywhere in the document to exit Microsoft Graph

 close GCReport01.doc

extra!

Understanding charts

Charts are made up of data markers grouped in series and data labels. A **data marker** represents a single piece of data—a number from the datasheet—in the chart. In this activity, the shorter bar over the Airport label in the chart is the data marker for the data in the first cell under the Airport column. A **data series** is the collection of all the data markers in a row or column in the datasheet. In this activity, the dark purple data markers make up the data series for the November data. A **data label** is text that identifies any part of the chart.

Figure 5-9: Graph and datasheet inserted into a document

Chart of placeholder data

Datasheet with placeholder data

Row 3 header

Column D header

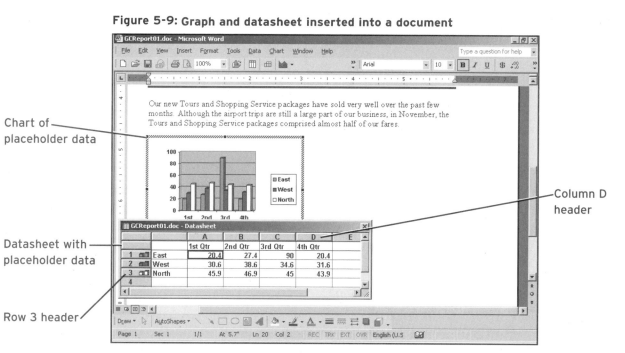

Figure 5-10: Completed datasheet

Airport data marker for October

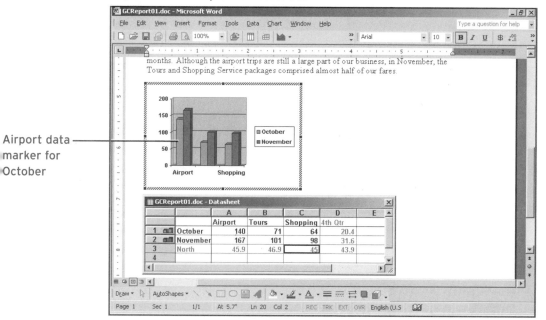

Skill Set 5

Working with Graphics

Create and Modify Diagrams and Charts
Modify a Chart

Once you have inserted a chart, you can modify it in several ways. For example, you can change the chart type, add labels, and resize the objects that make up the chart object. To format an object within a chart, make sure Microsoft Graph is open, click the chart to select it, then click the object in the chart that you want to format.

Activity Steps

 open GCReport02.doc

1. Scroll down to see the chart, then double-click the **chart** to open Microsoft Graph

2. Click the **Chart Type button list arrow** , then click the **Pie Chart button**

3. Double-click the **row 1 header** in the datasheet to exclude the October data and use only the November data in the pie chart
   See Figure 5-11.

4. Click **Chart** on the menu bar, then click **Chart Options** to open the Chart Options dialog box

5. Click the **Titles tab** if necessary, click in the **Chart title box**, type **November Fares**, click the **Data Labels tab**, click the **Percentage check box**, then click **OK**

6. Click anywhere in the chart area, position the pointer over the area just around the pie chart so that the ScreenTip says **Plot Area**, click to select the **Plot Area**, then drag the **sizing handles** to resize the pie chart so that it fills the left side of the chart object

7. Right-click the **Plot Area**, click **Format Plot Area** on the shortcut menu, click the **None option button** in the Border section to remove the border around the Plot Area, then click **OK**

8. Click outside of the **chart object** to close Microsoft Graph, click the chart object to select it, click the **Center button** , then click anywhere outside the chart to deselect the object
   See Figure 5-12.

close GCReport02.doc

tip

You can close the datasheet by clicking its Close button and reopen it by clicking Datasheet on the View menu.

Figure 5-11: Changing which data series is plotted in the pie chart

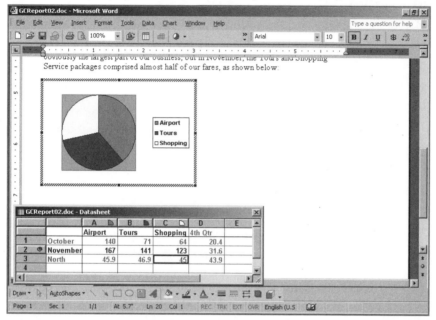

Figure 5-12: Modified chart

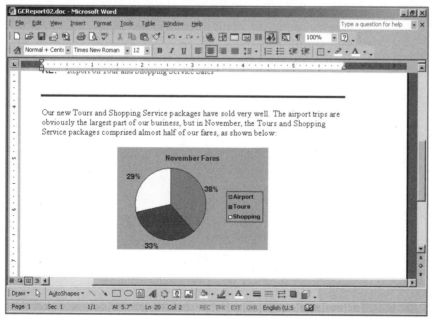

Skill Set 5
Working with Graphics

Create and Modify Diagrams and Charts
Add and Format Objects in a Chart

You can format almost any object in a chart individually. You can add labels to the axes, change the font of labels, add formatting to numbers on the chart, and add objects to your chart to enhance it.

Activity Steps

 open GCMemo06.doc

1. Scroll down to see the chart, double-click the chart to open Microsoft Graph, then click the **Close button** ⊠ in the datasheet title bar

2. Right-click any label on the vertical axis, click **Format Axis** on the shortcut menu, then click the **Number tab**

3. Click **Currency** in the Category list, click the **Decimal places down arrow** twice to change it to 0, then click **OK**

4. Click **Chart** on the menu bar, click **Chart Options**, click the **Titles tab** if necessary, click in the **Value (Z) axis box**, type **Total Sales**, click the **Legend tab**, click the **Show legend check box** to deselect it, then click **OK**

5. Right-click **Total Sales**, click **Format Axis Title**, click the **Alignment tab**, double-click in the Degrees box, type **90**, then click **OK**

6. If the Drawing toolbar is not visible, click the **Drawing button** , click the **Arrow button** on the Drawing toolbar, then drag down to draw an arrow pointing to the top of the **Apr** data point as shown in Figure 5-13

7. Click the **Text Box button** on the Drawing toolbar, click above the **Apr** data point, click the **Font size list arrow** 11 ▾, click **9**, then type **Easter sales increase**

8. Click anywhere in the document to close Microsoft Graph
   See Figure 5-14.

 close GCMemo06.doc

Step 7
If the text box you inserted is in the wrong place, drag it by its edge. If the text box is not large enough, drag a sizing handle.

Figure 5-13: Adding an arrow object to a chart

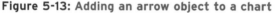

ow
ect

matted
label

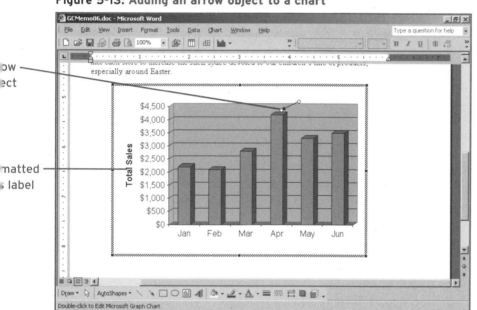

Figure 5-14: Chart with formatted objects

box

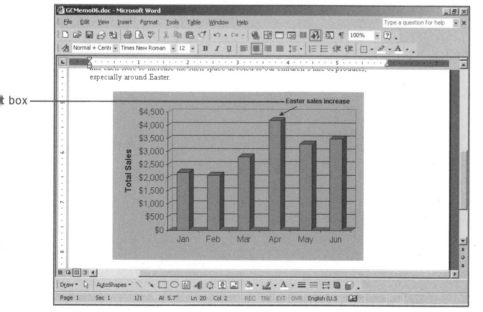

extra!

Understanding objects

An object is anything that can be manipulated—resized, dragged, recolored—as a unit. In this activity, once the chart was inserted into the document, it became a chart object, and Word treats it as one element. You can right-click the object, then use the Format Object command to change characteristics about the object, such as its fill color. Also, it's important to understand that many objects are made up of smaller objects. When you work with the chart in Microsoft Graph, you can manipulate individual components of the chart, such as the legend or the axis labels. Each of these components is an object.

Skill Set 5
Working with Graphics

Target Your Skills

 GCMemo07.doc

1 Modify the **GCMemo07** file to create the final document shown in Figure 5-15. To format the organizational chart, first choose a diagram style, then modify individual components as needed. (*Hint*: To format the connecting lines, click the Select button on the Organization Chart toolbar, then click All Connecting Lines.)

Figure 5-15

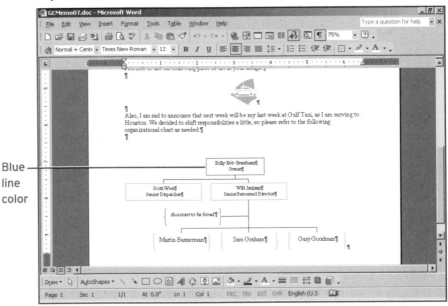

Blue line color

GCAnnouncement04.doc

2 Modify the **GCAnnouncement04** file to create the document shown in Figure 5-16. The image at the top of the document is in the **GCTaxiLogo02.bmp** file. Create the chart with the following tours and numbers of tours sold: **Galveston State Park, 120; Seawolf Park, 50; Moody Gardens, 45;** and **Pier 21, 30.**

Figure 5-16

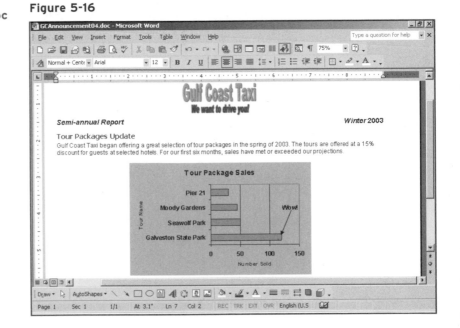

Skill Set 6
Workgroup Collaboration

Skill List

1. Compare and merge documents
2. Insert, view, and edit comments
3. Convert documents into Web pages

Word has several features and commands that make it easy to share information with others. For example, when you create a document, you might want to make changes based on someone else's input. In Skill Set 6, you will learn how to compare and merge two versions of the same document. You will also learn how to insert, view, and edit comments in your documents.

Posting a document on the Web is an easy way to make it available to others. You can do this easily by saving a Word document as a Web page. You will learn how to do this and how to preview the Web page before you save it.

Skill Set 6
Workgroup Collaboration

Compare and Merge Documents

Sometimes you need to get another person's opinion on a document you create. Someone else can open your document and make changes, then you can use the Compare and Merge command to see all the changes clearly shown on the screen. See Table 6-1 for a list of the three ways you can merge documents. Once you've created the merged document, you can display or print it with the changes showing or with all the changes made but hidden. You can also display or print the original document with the changes showing (which looks slightly different than the merged document, but the results are the same) or without any changes made at all.

Activity Steps

 open EWProductInfo01.doc,
EWProductInfo02.doc

1. Make sure the **EWProductInfo02** project file, the edited document, is the current document, click **Tools** on the menu bar, then click **Compare and Merge Documents**

2. Locate and click the **EWProductInfo01** project file, then click the **Merge list arrow**
   See Figure 6-1.

3. Click **Merge into new document**

4. Click in the **Zoom box**, type **90**, press **[Enter]**, then scroll down, if necessary, so that all of the changes are visible on your screen

5. Position the insertion point over the word **Peppermint** in the first header to see the ScreenTip that identifies the person who made the change
   See Figure 6-2.

6. Click the **Display for Review list arrow** Final Showing Markup ▾ on the Reviewing toolbar that opened, then click **Final** to see the result of all the changes

7. Click the **Display for Review list arrow** Final Showing Markup ▾ on the Reviewing toolbar, then click **Original Showing Markup** to revert to the original marked-up document

8. Right-click any toolbar, then click **Reviewing** to close the Reviewing toolbar

 close EWProductInfo01.doc,
EWProductInfo02.doc

Step 3
Another way to merge the documents into a new document is to click the Legal blackline check box in the Compare and Merge dialog box, then click Compare.

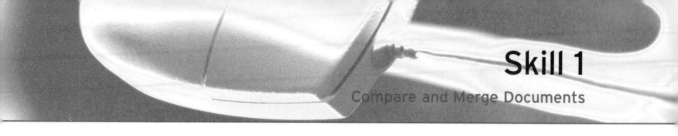

Figure 6-1: Compare and Merge Documents dialog box

Merge list arrow

Figure 6-2: New document created by merging documents

Name of person who made changes and date and time edits were made

Pointer

Text inserted into original document

Identifies deletion to original document

Identifies formatting change to original document

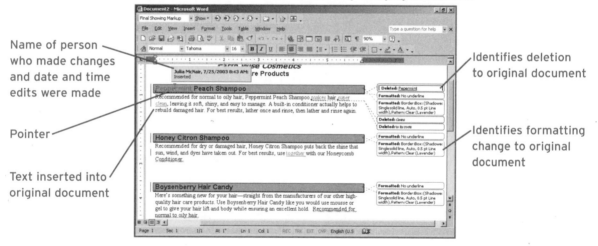

TABLE 6-1: Three ways to merge documents

command	best used for
Merge	Merges the changes into the original document and opens the original document if it's not already open
Merge into current document	Merges the changes into the edited (current) document
Merge into new document	Merges the changes into a new document and leaves the original and edited documents unchanged; clicking the Legal blackline check box and then clicking Compare produces the same result

Skill Set 6
Workgroup Collaboration

Insert, View, and Edit Comments
Insert and View Comments

Comments are notes that you add to a document. They are not printed with the document unless you specifically want them to be, but they are easily displayed on screen. In Print Layout and Web Layout view, comments are visible in Comment balloons, but you can hide them if you wish. You can also view comments in the Reviewing pane, a pane that you can open at the bottom of the window.

To see the names of all the people who have inserted comments in a document, click the Show button on the Reviewing toolbar, then point to Reviewers.

Activity Steps

 open EWBrochure05.doc

1. Position the insertion point immediately before **and chemicals** in the first line under the first heading

2. Click **Insert** on the menu bar, then click **Comment** to open a Comment balloon and the Reviewing toolbar
   See Figure 6-3.

3. Type **Mention UV rays** in the Comment balloon

4. Drag the horizontal scroll bar to the left if necessary, position the insertion point after **over-worked** in the first paragraph, click the **New Comment button**  on the Reviewing toolbar, then type **Delete "over-worked"** in the Comment balloon
   See Figure 6-4.

5. Click the **Show button** Show ▾ on the Reviewing toolbar, then click **Comments** to hide the Comment balloons

6. Click the **Show button** Show ▾ on the Reviewing toolbar, then click **Reviewing Pane** to display the Reviewing pane

7. Click the **Show button** Show ▾ on the Reviewing toolbar, click **Comments** to display the Comment balloons again, click the **Show button** Show ▾ , then click **Reviewing Pane** to close the Reviewing pane

8. Right-click any toolbar, then click **Reviewing** to close the Reviewing toolbar

 close EWBrochure05.doc

Figure 6-3: Comment balloon and Reviewing toolbar opened

Reviewing toolbar may be in a different position on your screen

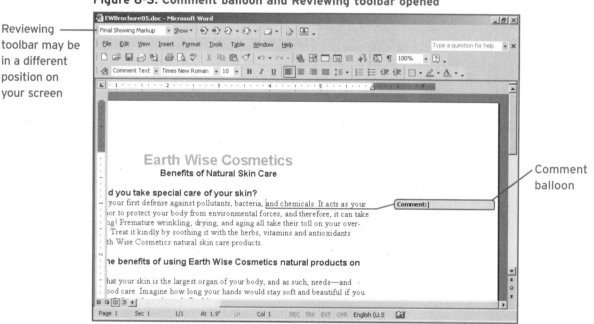

Comment balloon

Figure 6-4: Comments entered in document

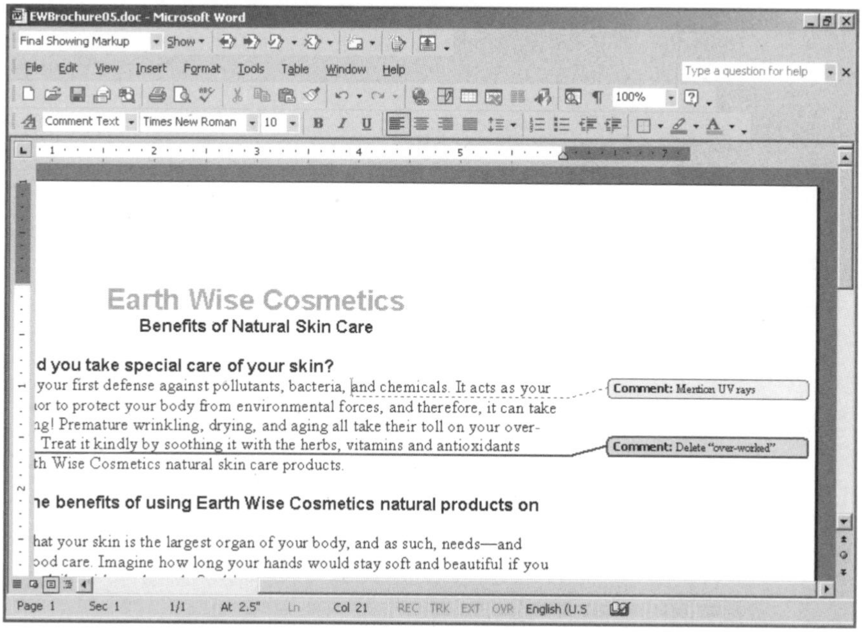

Skill Set 6
Workgroup Collaboration

Insert, View, and Edit Comments
Edit Comments

Once you've entered comments into a document, you can edit or delete them just like regular text. You can do this in each Comment balloon or in the Reviewing pane.

To print comments in a document, select Document showing markup in the Print what list in the Print dialog box. To print only comments, select List of markup in the Print what list.

Activity Steps

 open EWPriceList01.doc

1. Click **View** on the menu bar, point to **Toolbars**, then click **Reviewing** to open the Reviewing toolbar, if necessary

2. Click the **Next button** on the Reviewing toolbar to move to the next comment in the document

3. Double-click **deluxe** in the selected comment, then type **luxury**

4. Click the **Next button** on the Reviewing toolbar

5. Click the **Reject Change/Delete Comment button** on the Reviewing toolbar
   See Figure 6-5.

6. Right-click any toolbar, then click **Reviewing** to close the Reviewing toolbar

close EWPriceList01.doc

Figure 6-5: Document with edited comments

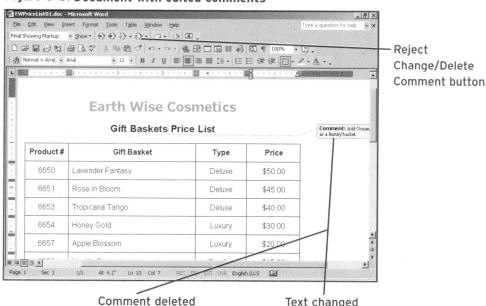

Reject Change/Delete Comment button

Comment deleted

Text changed

extra!

Changing the size and appearance of comments

You can change the way tracked comments look in the Comment balloons and in the Reviewing pane. To change the size of the text in the Comment balloons and in the Reviewing pane, click the Next button on the Reviewing toolbar to select a Comment balloon, open the Styles and Formatting task pane, click the list arrow next to Comment Text under Formatting of selected text, click Modify, then change the options in the dialog box. To change the size of the Comment balloons, click Options on the Tools menu, then click the Track Changes tab. Change the width in the Preferred width box under Use balloons in Print and Web Layout.

Skill Set 6
Workgroup Collaboration

Convert Documents into Web Pages
Preview and Save Documents as Web Pages

Publishing a document on the Web or a company intranet is an easy way to make it accessible to a wide audience. Before you save a document as a Web page, you should preview it to make sure that it looks the way you expect it to. After previewing the Web page, you use the Save as Web Page command to automatically save a copy of the document in the HTML file format, a file format that Web browsers use to display pages.

Step 5
The Web page title appears in the title bar of the browser window when the page is being viewed. It also appears in the browser's history list and would appear on a favorite or book-mark list if someone saves the link to the page.

Activity Steps

 open EWChart01.doc

1. Click **File** on the menu bar, then click **Web Page Preview**
2. Click the **Maximize button** ▣ in your Web browser window, if necessary
3. Click the **Close button** ☒ in your Web browser window
4. Click **File** on the menu bar, then click **Save as Web Page** to open the Save As dialog box
5. Click **Change Title**, press [➡], press the [Spacebar], type **Aromatherapy Best Sellers**, then click **OK**
6. Select all of the text in the File name box, then type **My Web Page**
   See Figure 6-6.
7. Click **Save** to close the Save As dialog box, and view the HTML document in Web Layout view
   See Figure 6-7.

 close EWChart01.doc

Figure 6-6: Save As dialog box for saving a document as a Web page

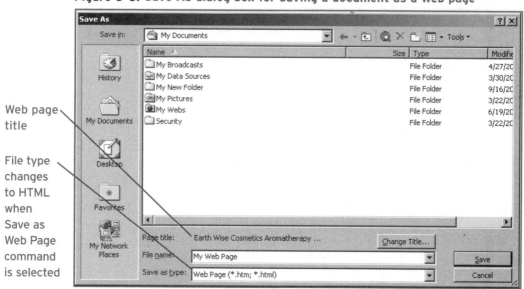

Web page title

File type changes to HTML when Save as Web Page command is selected

Figure 6-7: Document converted to a Web page in Web Layout view

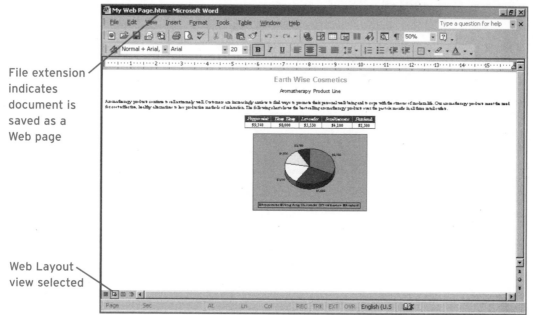

File extension indicates document is saved as a Web page

Web Layout view selected

Skill Set 6

Workgroup Collaboration

Target Your Skills

 EWProductInfo03.doc
EWProductInfo04.doc

1 Use Figure 6-8 as a guide for creating a new merged document. In addition to the changes in the figure, delete the comment **Will this be manufactured next year?** After you have created the final document, select Final in the Display for Review list. Close the Reviewing toolbar when you are finished.

Figure 6-8

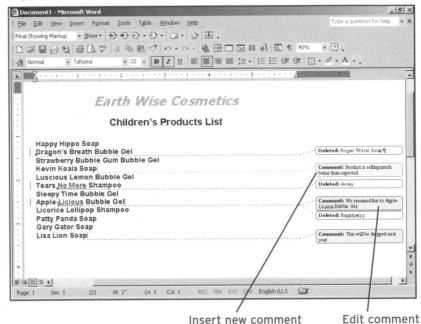

Insert new comment   Edit comment

 EWPriceList02.doc

2 Use Figure 6-9 as a guide to create the Web page shown. Note that the Web page in the figure is in a browser window, but you will end up with an HTML document displayed in Web Layout view in Word. Make sure you change the Web page title to match the one shown in the title bar in the figure.

Figure 6-9

Web page title

Filename

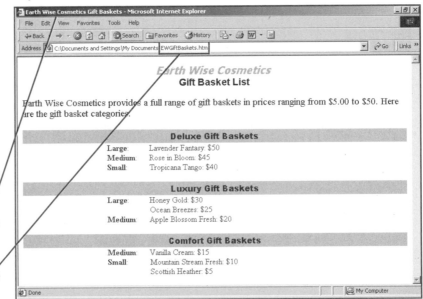

Word 2002 Core Projects Appendix

Projects List

Project 1 – Meeting Minutes for Mariposa Community Center

Project 2 – Advertising Bulletin for Skis 'n Boards

Project 3 – Newsletter for the Marine Educational Foundation

Project 4 – Memo for Lakeland Art Gallery

Project 5 – Information Sheet for Classic Car Races

Project 6 – Web Page for Allure Cosmetics

The Word Core skill sets cover a broad range of formatting and file management skills. Once you have mastered these skills, you can create many different document types. In the following projects, you will format a set of meeting minutes, an advertising bulletin, and a newsletter. You will also create a memo from one of Word's preset templates, add graphics to an information sheet, and save a Word document as a Web page that you can post to a Web site on the World Wide Web.

Project for Skill Set 1

Inserting and Modifying Text

Meeting Minutes for Mariposa Community Center

Each month a different staff member at the Mariposa Community Center in Carmel, California is responsible for recording the minutes of the monthly staff meeting. As the Office Manager at the Center, you receive and format each month's set of minutes before printing them for distribution to all staff. For this project, you will edit and format the minutes of the May 2004 meeting.

Activity Steps

 open WC_Project1.doc

1. Change **Mara Ramon** to **Darryl Cook** in the first bulleted item

2. Use the Find and Replace function to replace every instance of **Manjit Sidhu** with **Mitra Biazar**

3. Replace the second '**e**' in Hélene with **è** (in the bulleted item under "France Exchange Program")

4. Copy **report** in the first bullet under Fundraising Committee Report, use Paste Special to paste it after **Recreation Council** as unformatted text, capitalize **report**, then cut **Recreation Council Report** and its accompanying bulleted items and paste it below **Other Committee Reports**

5. Format the text **Mariposa Community Center** at the top of the page with **Bold**, then remove **Italics** from **Gym Fitness Program Builder** (in the first bulleted item below "Director's Report")

6. Use spell check to correct the spelling errors "**brekfast**" and "**oportunities**" and the grammatical error in the second bulleted item under Other Committee Reports
   Note that you should ignore the correction to "Mitra Biazar."

7. Enhance the text **May Meeting Minutes** with the Shadow font effect, then highlight the two names in the first bulleted item with **Turquoise**

8. Insert and center the current date below May Meeting Minutes; ensure the date is set to update automatically

9. Change the format of the date you just inserted to use the format that corresponds with **May 2, 2004**

10. Apply the Pacific character style to the text Pacific Marathon Boosters Association (under the Other Committee Reports heading)
    The completed minutes appear as shown in Figure WP 1-1.

Step 3
To insert the è symbol, click Insert on the menu bar, click Symbol, select the (normal text) font, click è, click Insert, then click Close.

 close WC_Project1.doc

Figure WP 1-1: Completed minutes for Mariposa Community Center

Mariposa Community Center
May Meeting Minutes
May 2, 2004

Approval of Minutes
- Minutes from the April 2004 meeting were approved by Darryl Cook and seconded by Mitra Biazar

Fundraising Committee Report – Barry Deville
- Barry circulated a report on fundraising activities. The report provided information about the following topics:
  - Organizing a large fund-raising committee for the summer of 2004
  - Organizing a bingo night in partnership with Mitra Biazar, the Director of Athletics
  - Learning about the Charitable You Club, a local charity fundraising company

Other Committee Reports
P.M.B.A. (*Pacific Marathon Boosters Association*)
- The next run event will be held on June 2 and will include a marathon, a 10K fun run, and a 5K walk/run. The cost of the run will be $30.00, which includes a T-shirt, a hat, OR a water bottle.
- Tim Simmons, a world champion marathoner, will hold a Marathon Clinic on May 20. All registrants for the June 2 marathon are encouraged to attend.
- The next P.M.B.A. meeting is June 5, 2004.

Recreation Council Report
- The breakfast held for fitness instructors on Instructor Appreciation Day was a success
- The gym equipment committee will be cleaning and restoring equipment during the week of May 24 to May 31. Volunteers are requested.

France Exchange Program
- Marie-Hélène Rousseau will host a meeting for parents and students interested in participating in the 9th Annual France-California Exchange. This year, students will spend three weeks in the Loire Valley.

Director's Report
- The Professional Development day on May 1 was successful. Recreation instructors learned how to use the new Gym Fitness Program Builder to upload fitness information to the Mariposa Community Center Web site.
- A new large group room will be located in the lower hallway on the 200 floor. Multimedia presentations can be given in the room to audiences of up to 75 people.
- The post-secondary evening held on May 5 was fully attended. Parents and students from the area's high schools attended a lively presentation about career and educational opportunities.

Project for Skill Set 2

Creating and Modifying Paragraphs

Advertising Bulletin for Skis 'n Boards

Skis 'n Boards is a ski and snowboarding shop with three outlets in the Vancouver area. To celebrate the start of the ski season, each outlet will host a snowboarding demonstration given by two world-class snowboarders from International Snowboarding, the premier manufacturer of snowboarding equipment. The demonstrations will take place on three consecutive Saturdays in November at each of the three Skis 'n Boards outlets. You've been given a Word document containing a bulletin that advertises the event. Now you need to format the bulletin attractively so that each Skis 'n Boards outlet can distribute copies to customers, media people, and local businesses. The completed bulletin appears as shown in Figure WP 2-1.

Activity Steps

open WC_Project2.doc

1. Apply the **Heading 1** style to the document heading **Snowboard Demo!**, increase the font size to **28 pt**, then center the heading

2. Apply the **Heading 3** style to the entire first paragraph

3. Indent the first paragraph **.5"** from both the left and the right margins of the page, apply the **Justified** alignment, then select **1.5 line spacing** for the first paragraph
   You can make all these changes in the Paragraph dialog box.

4. Apply **Gray-10% shading** to the entire first paragraph

5. Select the paragraph that begins "Two awesome world-class boarders...", then apply the same formatting you applied to the first paragraph

6. Select the line containing Day, Date, and Location, open the Tabs dialog box, clear all the current tabs, set **Center tabs** at **.9"**, **2.6"**, and **4.6"**, click to the left of Day, press **[Tab]** to position the three headings, then enhance the three headings with **Bold**

7. Select the information about the three locations, use the ruler bar to set **Left tabs** at **.5"**, **2"**, and **4"**, then indent the three lines to the first tab stop
   The .5 stop appears halfway between the left margin and the 1 on the ruler bar.

8. Apply bullets in the style shown in Figure WP 2-1 to the text that describes the events at each Snowboarding Demo

9. Use the Increase Indent button to indent the bulleted text to the 1" tab stop, then double-space the text

close WC_Project2.doc

Step 6
To set tabs, click Format on the menu bar, click Tabs, click Clear All, type the required position, click the Center option button, then click Set. Type and set the remaining positions, then click OK.

Figure WP 2-1: Completed bulletin for Skis 'n Boards

Snowboard Demo!

Don't miss the Snowboard Demo at your local Skis 'n Boards outlet. You can also meet the Ski Bunny and win one of ten all-day lift tickets for Whistler-Blackcomb!

Day	Date	Location
Saturday	November 13, 2004	West Vancouver store
Saturday	November 20, 2004	Lonsdale Avenue store
Saturday	November 27, 2004	Kerrisdale store

Two awesome world-class boarders from International Snowboarding will be on hand to share tips and tricks while they perform an awesome series of stunts in our simulated half pipe. Each Snowboard Demo kicks off at noon. Here's an outline of events:

- Noon: The Ski Bunny mascot arrives to greet shoppers and pose for pictures
- 12:30: International Snowboarding experts Maury White and Adam Schreck arrive and sign autographs
- 1:00: First half pipe demo
- 1:30   Break; entertainment provided by the Powder Blues Band
- 2:00   Second half pipe demo
- 2:30   Maury and Adam sign autographs
- 3:00   Drawing for 10 discount lift tickets

Project for Skill Set 3

Formatting Documents

Newsletter for the Marine Educational Foundation

You work part-time in the administrative office of the Marine Educational Foundation, a non-profit educational organization that offers courses in marine ecology from its residential facility in Marathon, Florida. Your supervisor has just e-mailed you a copy of the Fall 2004 Newsletter and asked you to format it over two pages so it appears as shown in Figure WP 3-1 on pages 7 and 9.

Activity Steps

 open WC_Project3a.doc

1. Change the orientation of the document to **Portrait**, then change the left and right margins to 1"

2. Format the text from **2004 Educational Programs** to the end of the document in **two columns** of equal width

3. Remove the current header, then create a footer containing **your name** at the left margin and a **page number** at the right margin

4. Click below the first paragraph in the 2004 Education Programs topic, create a table containing **seven rows** and **two columns**, then enter and format the text as shown in Figure WP 3-1

5. Apply the **Table Contemporary** AutoFormat to the table in the Leadership Programs section, remove the row containing information about **Angus Marsh**, insert a new column to the left of **State**, then enter the column head **Age** in bold and the ages of the students in the column cells, as shown in Figure WP 3-1

6. In the table in the Upcoming Educational Program section, change the Green shading to **Light Green**, then change the font color of the text to **Black**

7. Increase the width of column 1 to **3.2"**, insert a page break before the Upcoming Educational Programs section, clear the formatting to remove the Heading 1 style at the bottom of page 1, then balance the columns on Page 1

8. Insert a column break at the beginning of the second paragraph of the Annual Meeting section on Page 2, view the newsletter in Print Preview, then print a copy of the document

9. Create and print a sheet of labels containing the address of the Marine Educational Foundation shown on Page 2 of the newsletter, then save the labels as **WC_Project3b.doc**

 close WC_Project3a.doc
WC_Project3b.doc

Step 4
You will need to bold and center the text in Row 1, reduce the width of the columns, center the percentages in column 2, then center the table between the left and right margins of the newsletter column.
Step 7
To clear formatting, click the Styles list arrow on the Formatting toolbar, then click Clear Formatting.

Figure WP 3-1: Completed newsletter for Marine Educational Foundation

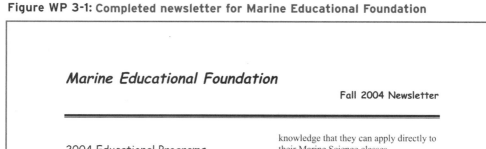

Marine Educational Foundation

Fall 2004 Newsletter

2004 Educational Programs

In 2004, the Marine Educational Foundation hosted 300 student groups from all over the United States in its marine educational programs. Over 1000 students learned about the history and ecology of the mangrove, coral reef, and grass bed systems of the Florida Keys. Most student groups were from the state of Florida, followed closely by students from California and then New York and Georgia. The following table shows the states from which the highest percentage of our student groups traveled in 2004.

State	Percent of Students
Florida	43%
California	19%
New York	13%
Georgia	13%
South Carolina	7%
New Jersey	5%

New Facility

In 2005, we will begin construction of a new facility near San Diego in California to provide our west coast students with an ecological experience more related to their home environment.

Our members recognize the benefits of combining travel with study. The students who attend the Marine Educational Foundation enjoy a unique travel experience, while gaining knowledge that they can apply directly to their Marine Science classes.

Web Presence

Increasingly, our Web site is attracting interest from students and educators outside the United States. In 2005, we plan to expand our program to include students from Canada, England, Germany, Japan, and Brazil. Check out our site at: www.marinedfoundation.com.

Leadership Programs

The table shown below lists the students who participated in a special leadership group that was run at the Marine Educational Foundation in June 2004. The students were chosen on the basis of their teamwork skills, leadership potential, and academic achievement. The three-day program was a great success.

Last Name	First Name	Age	State
Amin	Zahra	16	CA
Flynn	Kate	17	NY
Leblanc	Michel	16	NY
McGraw	Andy	16	NJ
Penner	Marike	18	PA
Ramirez	Teresa	18	FL
Sanchez	Juan	17	FL
Yeung	Martha	17	CA

[Your Name]

1

Figure WP 3-1 (continued): Completed newsletter for Marine Educational Foundation

Upcoming Educational Programs

We are anticipating the best season ever in the Spring of 2000 as over five-hundred groups are scheduled to go through the program! Here's the list of programs offered in 2005:

Study	Price
Mangroves, Coral Reefs, and Grass Beds	$300
Mangroves 3-days	$100
Coral Reefs 3-days	$100
Grass Beds 3-days	$100
Coral Reefs, Dolphins Plus	$200
Save the Manatee	$75
Grass Beds and Coral Reefs	$200

All programs, except for those listed as 3-day, last for five days and do not include the cost of transportation from the student's home town to Marathon, Florida. The program price includes all meals, books, transportation, and dormitory-style accommodation while students are participating in the programs.

Annual Meeting

On October 23 at 5 p.m., the Marine Educational Foundation will host its annual meeting and member get-together! As always, we will hold the meeting at the Marine Educational Foundation site in Marathon, Florida. We hope to see some new faces this year, so bring along your friends. For out-of-town members, we're offering a special weekend rate at one of our local hotels of $180 for two nights. You can also enjoy the gourmet delights of our student cafeteria. It's a deal you just can't pass up! Check out the beautiful Florida Keys! If you want to take advantage of this special offer, please call Mark at (305) 872-6641.

Our agenda for this year's meeting is as follows:

- Welcome to New Members
- Budget Report
- Detailed Program Schedule for 2005
- Slide Presentation by Scott Smith on his 2004 Teaching Experience
- New Business
- Adjournment
- Party Time!

We're counting on seeing all the Marine Educational Foundation members this year!

Marine Educational Foundation
P.O. Box 41
Marathon, Florida 33051

[Your Name]

2

Project for Skill Set 4

Managing Documents

Memo for Lakeland Art Gallery

You've just been hired as an Administrative Assistant at the Lakeland Art Gallery on the shores of Georgian Bay in Ontario. One of your first duties is to create a memo describing the upcoming winter exhibition of gallery artists. You decide to base the memo on a template and then create a new folder to contain the memos you create for the gallery. You'll also save the memo in Text (.txt) format so you can distribute it to artists who use other word processing programs that may not be compatible with Word 2002.

Activity Steps

1. Click **General Templates** in the New Document task pane, click the **Memos tab** in the Templates dialog box, then select the **Contemporary Memo** template

2. Modify the template so the completed memo appears as shown in Figure WP 4-1

3. Open the Save As dialog box, then create a new folder called **Art Gallery Memos**

4. Save the document as **WC_Project4.doc** in the Art Gallery Memos folder

5. Modify the document by changing the name of **Flora Wong** to **Flora Leung**

6. Save the changes to the document, then close the document

7. Open **WC_Project4.doc**, save the document in Plain Text (.txt) format with the default settings, then close the document

8. Open the **WC_Project4.txt** file
   Note that you'll need to click the Files of type list arrow and select All Files to see the .txt file.

   close WC_Project4.txt

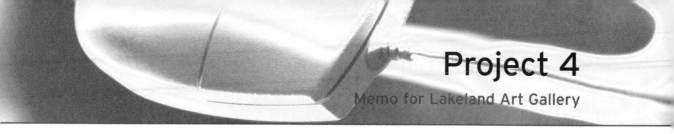

Figure WP 4-1: Completed memo for Lakeland Art Gallery

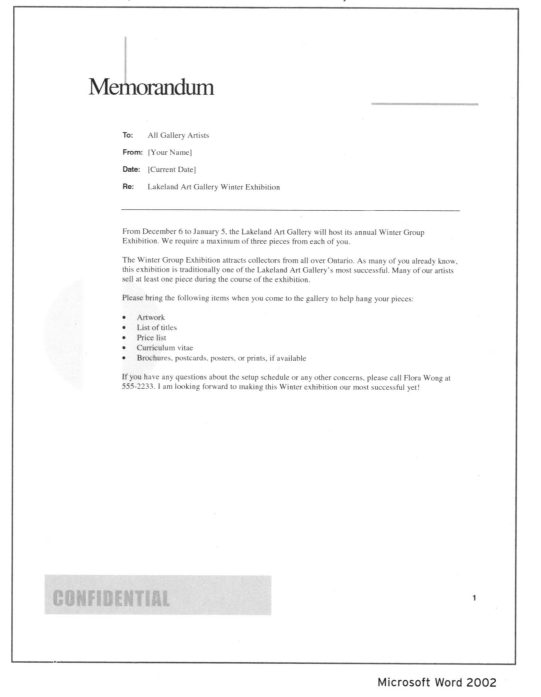

Memorandum

To: All Gallery Artists

From: [Your Name]

Date: [Current Date]

Re: Lakeland Art Gallery Winter Exhibition

From December 6 to January 5, the Lakeland Art Gallery will host its annual Winter Group Exhibition. We require a maximum of three pieces from each of you.

The Winter Group Exhibition attracts collectors from all over Ontario. As many of you already know, this exhibition is traditionally one of the Lakeland Art Gallery's most successful. Many of our artists sell at least one piece during the course of the exhibition.

Please bring the following items when you come to the gallery to help hang your pieces:

- Artwork
- List of titles
- Price list
- Curriculum vitae
- Brochures, postcards, posters, or prints, if available

If you have any questions about the setup schedule or any other concerns, please call Flora Wong at 555-2233. I am looking forward to making this Winter exhibition our most successful yet!

CONFIDENTIAL

1

Project for Skill Set 5

Working with Graphs

Information Sheet for Classic Car Races

The Adirondacks Raceway hosts a series of races for owners of classic sports racing cars of the 1950's and 1960's. As the Office Manager of the facility, you decide to create an information sheet for prospective racers. The sheet includes a pie chart, a clip art picture, a photograph of a classic car, and a diagram showing the steps required to register for a classic car race. The two pages of the completed information sheet appear in Figure WP 5-1 on pages 11 and 13.

Step 3
After you create the default column chart, click Chart on the menu bar, click Chart Type, click Pie, then click OK. You will then need to click Data on the Menu bar and then click Series in Columns.

Activity Steps

 open WC_Project5.doc

1. Insert the picture file called **Ferrari.jpg** at the beginning of paragraph 1, then change the layout to **Square**

2. Use your mouse to size and position the picture in paragraph 1 as shown in Figure WP 5-1

3. Create a **pie chart** that includes a legend from the data in the table, then delete the table

4. Increase the size of the pie chart and center it, as shown in Figure WP 5-1, double-click the **chart**, click just the **grey background** behind the pie, then press **[Delete]**

5. Insert, size, and position the **clip art image** shown in Figure WP 5-1
   Search for "racing car" in the Microsoft Clip Gallery. You will need to be online to access the full Microsoft Clip Gallery. If you are not able to go online, use another similar image of a car from the Microsoft Clip Gallery.

 close WC_Project5.doc

Project 5

Information Sheet for Classic Car Races

Figure WP 5-1: Completed information sheet for Classic Car Races

Adirondacks Raceway
Classic Sports Racing Car Competition

The Adirondacks Raceway located outside Saratoga Springs, New York hosts five classic sports racing car competitions each season. Drivers who own some of the most beautiful classic racing cars of the 1950's and 60's relive the glory days of racing, when the sleek design and ear-shattering power of front engine sports cars ruled the raceways. Famed drivers of the times make regular appearances to the delight of their many fans.

The pie chart shown below displays the breakdown of race winners over the past three years by car type.

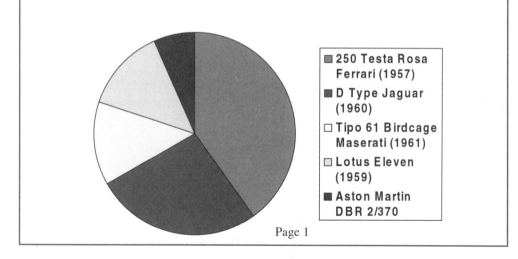

- 250 Testa Rosa Ferrari (1957)
- D Type Jaguar (1960)
- Tipo 61 Birdcage Maserati (1961)
- Lotus Eleven (1959)
- Aston Martin DBR 2/370

Page 1

Microsoft Word 2002   **181**

Project for Skill Set 6

Workgroup Collaboration

Web Page for Allure Cosmetics

Allure Cosmetics owns several shops in New Zealand. The company's rich, multi-scented soaps, gels, lotions, and cosmetics have become justly famous throughout the country. Now you and your colleagues are working on transforming existing marketing documents for use on the company's new Web site. In this project you will work on a description of the company's three top-selling cleansing products and insert a comment for your colleague, Joanne Plaice. You will then merge the document with another version edited by Joanne to produce a final copy that incorporates your comment and Joanne's comments and changes. Finally, you will save the document as a Web page and view it in your browser. Figure WP 6-1 shows the merged version of the document with two sets of comments.

Activity Steps

 open WC_Project6A.doc
WC_Project6B.doc

1. In the WC_Project6A document, select **Mango Cleansing Milk**, insert a comment with the text **What do you think of changing the name to Mango Wash?**, then save and close the document

2. In the WC_Project6B document, view the two comments inserted by Joanne

3. Merge to a new document the WC_Project6B document with the WC_Project6A document

4. Save the new document as **WC_Project6C.doc**, then print a copy
Figure WP 6-1 shows how the merged document appears when printed.

5. In response to the three comments, change the name of Mango Cleansing Milk to **Mango Wash** (two places), change tropical dawn to **tropical evening**, then change cool water to **warm water**

6. Use the appropriate buttons on the Reviewing toolbar to accept all the changes in the document, then delete all the comments in the document

7. Save the document as a Web page called **WC_Project6D.htm**, apply the Watermark theme, then view the document in your Web browser
Figure WCP 6-2 shows how the document appears in the browser.

 close WC_Project6B.doc
WC_Project6C.doc
WC_Project6D.htm

Figure WP 6-1: Merged document

Allure Cosmetics - Microsoft Internet Explorer

Back | Links | Customize Links | Address | A:\\WC_Project6D.htm | Go

File Edit View Favorites Tools Help

Allure Cosmetics
Cleansing Products

Mango Wash

Recommended for Normal to Oily Skin, the Mango Wash provides your face with a lightly scented wash that will remove make-up and excess oil to leave the skin as soft and fresh as a tropical evening. Massage the cleanser into your face once each evening before bed.

Rose Soap Gel

Recommended for Normal to Dry Skin, our Rose Soap Gel will clean and nourish your skin with a mildly astringent, oil-free gel. Massage the gel gently into your face twice a day and then rinse well with warm water.

Citrus Wash

Recommended for Oily Skin, the mildly astringent properties of our Citrus Wash are guaranteed to leave your skin as soft as a summer breeze. Use the wash each morning to wake yourself up and send you refreshed into a new day. Rinse well with warm water and then pat dry with an absorbent cloth.

Done | My Computer

Glossary

.doc filename extension that identifies a file as one created in Microsoft Word

.dot filename extension that identifies a Microsoft Word template file

.htm filename extension that identifies a file as a file created using HyperText Markup Language

.rtf filename extension that identifies a file saved in Rich Text Format

active document the current document; the document in which you are currently entering or editing text

cell the intersection of a row and column in a table or a datasheet

centered text or an object that is centered between the left and right margins

chart a visual representation of data in a datasheet

clip (clip art) a drawing, photograph, sound, or movie that you can insert into a document

clipboard an area in the computer in which cut and copied text is stored

comment notes that you add to a document that are not printed unless you specify that you want to print them

copy to place a duplicate of text or an object on the system or Office clipboard so that may be pasted into another location

cut to remove text or an object and store it on the system or Office clipboard so that may be pasted into another location

data label text that identifies any part of the chart

data marker the bar, column, or point that represents a single piece of data in a chart

data series the collection of all data markers in a row or column in a datasheet

datasheet rows and columns in which you enter data to be graphed in Microsoft Graph

docked toolbar a toolbar positioned along the edge of the screen

document a file that you create using a word-processing program

drawing canvas the area in a document in which a drawing or diagram is located

field a placeholder for something that might change in a document, such as the page number or the current date

filename extension three letters that follow a period after the filename; the extension identifies the file type, for example, the extension *.doc* identifies a file created using Word

floating toolbar a toolbar positioned in the middle of the screen

font the design of letters and numbers

font size the size of characters in a document

font style the way characters look, for example, bold, italic, or underlined

footer text that appears at the bottom of every page in a document

format the way something looks; the size, color, and style of a word or paragraph in a document

gutter margin the margin on the binding side of a document

hanging indent a paragraph in which all of the lines following the first line are indented a specified amount

header text that appears at the top of every page in a document

inactive document an open document in which you are not currently entering or editing text

insertion point the place on screen where the next character you type will appear

justified text text or an object aligned along both the left and right margins

landscape orientation a page set up to print sideways so that the page is wider than it is tall

left-aligned text text or an object aligned along the left margin

mirror margins inside and outside margins set up for odd and even pages

object an item that can be manipulated as a whole, for example, an image or a chart in a document

Office Clipboard the clipboard that comes with Office and can store up to 24 of the most recently cut or copied items from any Office program

organizational chart a graphical representation of a hierarchical structure

paste to copy into a document the text or object stored on the system or Office clipboard

pica a measurement for text equal to approximately 12 points

placeholder a section in a template that you can click once to select then type to replace the existing text

point (pt) measurement for text equal to approximately 1/72 of an inch

portrait orientation a page set up to print lengthwise so that the page is taller than it is wide

pt see *point*

right-aligned text text or an object aligned along the right margin

section parts of a document, usually differentiating various formats

select to highlight a word or words in a document; also, to click a command

smart tag a button that appears on screen when Word recognizes a word or phrase as belonging to a certain category, for example, a name or address

style a defined set of formats that you can apply to words or paragraphs

symbol a character not included in the standard English alphabet or Arabic numerals

system clipboard the clipboard that contains only the most recently cut or copied item

tab leader a dotted, dashed, or solid line before a tab stop

tab stop the location on the ruler where text moves when you press [Tab]

task pane a panel that appears along the left or right of the screen and contains a sets of related hyperlinks to program commands

template a set of styles and formats that determines how a particular type of document will look

toggle turn something on or off; make something, such as a command or toolbar button, active or inactive

toolbar a row of buttons that provide one-click access to frequently used commands

undo to automatically reverse the previous action by clicking the Undo command or button

view a way of looking at a document; Word offers four views: Normal, Print Layout, Outline, and Web Layout

wizard a series of dialog boxes in which you answer questions and choose options to customize a template

word-processing program a program that makes it easy to enter text and manipulate that text in documents

word-wrap the process where the insertion point automatically moves to the next line in a document when it reaches the end of a line

zoom magnification of the document on screen

Index

A

address book, using smart tags with, 18
animation. *See also* images
    text animation application, 54-55
Answer Wizard, 20. *See also* Help
AutoComplete feature. *See also* text
    using, 38-39
AutoCorrect feature. *See also* text
    adding words to, 19
    using, 40-41
AutoFormat. *See also* tables
    applying to tables, 116-117
AutoText entry. *See also* text
    creating, 38-39

B

.bmp file format, 146
bulleted list. *See also* list
    creating, 82-83
    customizing, 82

C

cell. *See also* tables
    in table, 112
        modifying, 122-123
character. *See also* text
    deleting, 28
    finding, 15
character effects, applying, 52-53
character formats
    applying, 42-43
    modifying, 44-45
character styles, applying, 62-63
chart
    creating, 152-153
        data label, 152
        data markers, 152
        data series, 152
        datasheet, 152
    diagram types, 151
    modifying, 154-155
    objects in, adding and formatting,
      156-157

    organizational chart
        creating, 148-149
        modifying, 150-151
clip art, inserting with Clip Organizer,
  144-145
Clip Organizer
    inserting images not stored in, 146-147
    inserting images stored in, 144-145
clipboard, 30. *See also* text
    Office Clipboard, 9
closing
    documents, 8-9
    without saving, 16
columns
    creating, 96-97
    creating before entering text, 100-101
    inserting and deleting in table, 120-121
    modify text alignment in, 98-99
    revise column layout, 102-103
comments
    editing, 164-165
    inserting and viewing, 162-163
copying. *See also* cutting and pasting text
    Paste Special command, 34-35
    pasting and, 32-33
cutting and pasting
    text, 30-31
        clipboard, 30

D

data label, 152. *See also* labels
data markers, 152
data series, 152
datasheet, 152. *See also* chart
date
    inserting, 58-59
    modifying date field, 39, 60-61
    using smart tags for, 18
deleting. *See also* character
    character, 28
.doc file extension, 2